D1733071

González projects his poetry in both Spanish and English, neither version being a translation of the other: it is the same poem. This is the essence of bilingualism, thinking simultaneously in two languages, living in two cultures. This is also the nature of the shaman, participating in a mental state which is not one but many personae. The result is a very haunting set of poems couched in images and language that are beautiful and universal. *'La piedra que late es perfecta—nada se mide=The stone that beats is perfect—nothing is measured; (Yollotl: Heart).'*

These verses do not simply exist in some archaic state as examples of pre-Columbian sensitivities, but are profoundly linked to González's ongoing concerns of peace and justice on earth today. The depth of his understanding of the archaic Nahua culture and the dilemmas that bedevil mankind today are demonstrated in a brilliant essay that concludes this book. For me, this collection represents the finest, the most beautiful poetry, both Chicano and cosmic, that I have encountered in some time. It's as if my twin José, Valum Votan, had come back in a new transformation. And this is poetry strengthened by the pressing social concerns that González so decisively challenges, in the great tradition of César Chávez."

IVÁN ARGÜELLES

"Someday, Rafael Jesús Gozález may well be recognized as the best poet of the twenty-first century. Richly metaphorical, stunningly well-crafted, profound, evocative, and quite simply beautiful, the fifty poems in his new collection *Chalchiuixochitl/Flor de Piedra Verde/Flower of Jade* spread before the reader a trilingual banquet in Nahuatl, Spanish, and English that recreates the mystical and religious lyricism of the Nahua (Aztecs), a culture almost obliterated by the Spanish who did their best to burn the Nahua's books and execute their priests, philosophers, and poets during the conquest of Mexico. Beginning by translating the fifteenth century poem '*Sueño de una palabra*/Dream of a Word' by Tecayehuatzin, Lord Huexotzinco, and ending with a long poem describing a descent into Mictlan (the Nahua underworld), González takes us to an ancestral space filled with dazzling symbols, a kindship with all living things, and a renewed sense of the 'sacredness of Life [and] of the Earth that birthed and sustained it.' As he warns in the poem 'In Xochitl in Cuicatl: Flower & Song': What most endures/is the flowering word. Without flower & song/the heart sleeps/... if we do not venerate/life & the Earth/ ... Spring will be silent, mute/ ... blind without the color of flowers./Love & sing it/for on our song/all depends.' No poet could have come along at a better time to remind us of the importance of these things, and few could have done it as well."

MARY MACKEY
author of *The Jaguars That Prowl Our Dreams*,
winner of the 2019 Eric Hoffer Award
for the Best Book Published by a Small Press

"Rafael Jesús González writes with the wisdom of age and with the wisdom of ages, yet his poems are fresh and timely. Nurtured by the past, the poet asks his readers, sons and daughters of corn, to be ready to fight against the greedy people (and multinational companies) who poison the sacred seed for their own profit in our present. *Chalchiuixochitl* brings back to life the indigenous philosophy and the aesthetics of Netzahualcoyotl and Tecayehuatzin, infusing them with the bilingual rhythms and sensibility of Chicano discourse. González, like the chalchiuhyollotl—the heart of green stone—blesses, names, and (fortunately for us) is not still!

In this collection of poems in the Nahua mode, Rafael Jesús González writes as if the world had just been created. González gets to name animals, objects, and concepts in an almost Adamic fashion. In bringing his readers back to that primordial, pre-Hispanic moment of endowing the world with meaning, González effects a substantial decolonizing process. The poet recovers and restores an alternative and powerful cognitive mode that rests on the power of metaphor to both describe and create reality. In doing so, González infuses new life into the nahua tradition with these poems written in both Spanish and English, a linguistic duality that mirrors and invokes the original dualism of Ometeotl, the male and female creator of the universe.

Rafael Jesús González escribe con la sabiduría de los años y de la historia, pero sus poemas son rabiosamente actuales. Inspirándose en el pasado indígena, el poeta pide a sus lectores (los hijos y las hijas del maíz) que estén listos para enfrentarse a los intereses egoístas de las multinacionales que envenenan la semilla sagrada para aumentar sus beneficios económicos. *Chalchiuixochitl* hace presente la filosofía y la estética de Netzahualcoyotl y Tecayehuatzin, impregnándolas con los ritmos y la sensibilidad bilingüe del lenguaje de los chicanos. González, como el chalchiuhyollotl—el corazón de jade—bendice, nombra y (por fortuna para nosotros) no se calla.

En esta nueva colección de poemas al estilo nahua, Rafael Jesús González escribe como si el mundo estuviera recién creado. Tal y como si fuera un nuevo Adán, el poeta da nombre a los animales, objetos y conceptos y los describe en un lenguaje rico de sugerencias y connotaciones multiculturales. Mediante esta estrategia de retrotraer a sus lectores a un momento primordial prehispánico, González efectúa una profunda descolonización del significado y del significante. Para ello, el autor se apoya en la tradición metafórica de las culturas amerindias, una manera de entender el universo desde la fusión de lo mítico y lo estético. González bebe con gusto de esas fuentes y consigue darles nueva vida en estos poemas escritos tanto en español como en inglés, un dualismo lingüístico que nos evoca el papel central que toda dualidad tenía para el mundo de los nahuas, creado por su dios/diosa Ometeotl."

MANUEL M. MARTÍN-RODRÍGUEZ
University of California, Merced

"In this collection, specifically addressing pre-Hispanic Nahua poetry, Rafael Jesús Gonzalez writes from the inside out with an endearing humility as he enters the spirits of the earth, summoning their wisdom and inspiration. The spirits respond in their own voices; the nopal, the maize, the squash, the green stone; the gods of all life in their myriad forms. We hear their voices and we begin to experience that we are not separate from, and therefore do not have dominion over, this planet and its children. The symbolism of blooms issuing from the voice represent poetry and song, and they reach to the sun, the moon and the stars. They are carried on the breezes. Being firmly planted in the earth allows for this flight, the dividing membrane thins, and all beings breathe together. There are songs of longing, of loss, there are broken songs and songs of redemption...all invoking the presence of the gods, for gods are many and attend to the varying needs of their 'children.'

We enter these sacred moments, and the seeds of an ancient civilisation spring to life and bloom through Rafael's deep connection with and love of the traditions imbedded and held in his being. There is healing when one immerses oneself in the metaphoric teachings of the poetry...bringing a deeper perspective to the Nahua way. Rafael follows the ways, loyally, honouring the ancestors and gods in everything that he does. He is a champion for the healing and stewardship of our delicately balanced world, and in this collection we begin to understand our connections to each other, and to every living being.

These poems are a lesson, and Rafael a teacher."

B. L. P. SIMMONS

"As they echo ancient traditions, sending a profound knowledge into our modern ears, blending this with a contemporary sensibility, these beautiful poems are moving and sonorous, a gift to us all."

SUSAN GRIFFIN

author of *A Chorus of Stones*

"With wisdom, reverence, flowers, and song, Rafael Jesús González has created a gorgeous book for the ages. Each poem is a pair: Spanish and English; yet the English half is not a translation. It's more a transformation of the idea of the poem. In the first poem of the volume, there's a saying from the ancient Anahuac 'what is most precious/what most endures/is the flowering word.' Gonzalez' poems revere the spiritual and at the same time the ordinary made brilliant—whether the subject is music, song, dance, or the moon. He brings us a sea snail, seeds of a sunflower, opossum who steals an ember from the blaze of Lord Jaguar to bring fire to the earth. The poem that deserves special attention is the amazing final epic: 'Descent to Mictlan' (shamanic journey to the underworld) that ends with a plea to leave the underworld, to 'Go and pass on the blessing of life.' "

SUSAN TERRIS

author of *Familiar Tense*

"'Only thus can we create the new world,' Rafael Jesús González tells us, by tatting new feathers, forging new gold and forming jade out of the old histories and civilizations that undergird our present day. Each poem on this collection, in both Spanish and English, is a song, sung with Rafael's sonorous voice in mind—if you've had the good fortune to have attended a reading—as he endows us with the blessing of his voice even on paper. These obras are to be read or sung out loud—one need not have a melodic voice—the words will carry the notes for you. For me it was a revelation as well to savor the sense of the nahuatl that each poem calls upon to give us a kind of entrée into that ancient people, my ancestors I dare call them, at least culturally. He inspires a love for the vibrant lenguaje that nahuatl is: nearly every poem teaches us another bit of nahuatl. No doubt, Rafael is conversant with the ancients, intent on passing along their knowledge and his, and thus he is a teixcuitiani, a maestro, in his own right."

ARMANDO RENDÓN

editor/founder, *Somos en escrito Magazine*
a native of San Antonio, Texas,
the award-winning author of
The Adventures of Noldo books for young adults,
author of *Chicano Manifesto*

"There is something elemental and life-affirming in all these poems. The Spirits call us. The Ancestors breath is in every word as they teach us new ways to see, to live, to heal. How happy we are to inhabit the magical world of the storyteller, Rafael Jesús González, Maestro/Teacher, Shaman Brother, and to feel his affectionate, loving, authentic, and truthful embrace of all Sentient Life. But do not be deceived—he can also be the firm and wise father who sets us back on the path as we wander the byways of our distractions and the afflictions of our unbalanced lives. Gracias, Rafael, for this work, which offers us the Nahua vision which emboldens us and gives us courage as we travel to the Stars."

DENISE CHÁVEZ
Fronteriza activist, founder of Libros Para El Viaje
(a refugee, migrant, and asylum-seekers book donation initiative),
and author of the novels *The King and Queen of Comezón* and *Loving Pedro Infante*, among other works

"*Chalchiuixochitl/Flor de Piedra Verde/Flower of Jade* embodies the poetic wisdom of ancient Mexico, speaking through the same rich, deeply symbolic language of the ancient Nahua poets, decorated with flowers and feathers, eternal values, the fleetingness of life, jade and conch, friendship and death, obsidian and copal, truth, and love. With Spanish, Nahuatl, and English, Rafael brings together three languages, cultures, world views and poetic traditions. Rafael's poems are medicine ceremonies. You can hear the rattles and drums. When he speaks he is always encircled by other ancient Nahua poets, a sacred garland of shamans, offering their songs as spells of healing. He sings about the medicinal value of flowering words, the enduring poetry made from flower and song. To place it all into context, Rafael then shares the insights of the visionary scholars who rediscovered Nahua poetry and made its wonders accessible to the modern world. A wondrous and important book."

JOHN CURL
author of *Ancient American Poets*

"In his collection of poetry Rafael Jesús González presents us with an innovative and unique poetic style and syntax as he resurrects ancient Nahuatl 'Flor y Canto' a form of poetry both recited and written over hundreds of years by the ancient Nahuatl-speaking Mexicans. It is to this legacy that González has attached himself as a Chicano poet who has inherited a remarkable history. The book is a treatise on Nahuatl poetry that delves into soul of an ancient culture and brings to light how it valued and revered mother earth. Its nature-based societies were grounded on spiritual philosophical and cosmological foundations that insured a social order able to flourish for hundreds of years. Hence the title of his book invokes the beauty and ephemerality of the flower (poetry and creative expression) and the longevity of Jade (legacy of truth and wisdom).

González' poems often contrast the more integrated pre-conquest Nahuatl civilization with the destructive and brutal assaults by past and present empires of invasion, plunder, exploitation, and genocide that the original people of the Americas have long suffered. There is beauty here and there are also dire warnings 'if we do not venerate Life and Earth.'

There is much to learn about the ancestors of ancient Mexico in this book since González is a poet and also a teacher of Nahuatl thought and culture. Hence he is able to weave these elements elegantly into his writings that echo the poetic forms and themes of 'Flor y Canto'. Language is pivotal and most of his poems are written in three languages Nahuatl, English, and Spanish. Poems flow freely from one language to the next. This constant switching of lingual codes creates a flow connecting time (ancient to modern) and history (the trajectory of Chicanismo) and place (the geographical and geopolitical vastness of an indigenous continent: the 'Americas'). Even the book's table of contents appears to be a multilingual poem of Nahuatl symbols and concepts mixed with current issues and frameworks.

The themes of much of his poetry are rooted in the Nahuatl philosophical questions about time, death, nature, illusion, and the transient and transitory nature of life. He evokes the ancestral and shamanic energies within a context of modern day dilemmas of inhumanity, abuse of living things, self-destruction, and social and spiritual fragmentation.

González allows us to see Flor y Canto as a vast source of history, identity and meaning that values human existence. This is especially clear in his essay at the end of the book where he changes form from poet to scholar and excavates the power of an advanced ancient culture and their contributions to science, law, aesthetics, spirituality, and integration. From this standpoint he calls for a 'revolution' against the dehumanization of our totally materialistic social order towards a more human-centered, heart-centered society. In this way this book is a call for change, and a time to re-envision a new world that can reference an ancient blue print of human evolution for the future. González' urgent call is clear in the following:

'Love and Sing it
for on our song
all depends'"

NAOMI QUIÑÓNEZ

NOMADIC PRESS

OAKLAND
PHILADELPHIA
XALAPA

WWW.NOMADICPRESS.ORG

MASTHEAD
Founding Publisher
J. K. FOWLER

ASSOCIATE EDITOR
MICHAELA MULLIN

EDITOR
NOELIA CERNA

DESIGN
JEVOHN TYLER NEWSOME

MISSON STATEMENT Through publications, events, and active community participation, Nomadic Press collectively weaves together platforms for intentionally marginalized voices to take their rightful place within the world of the written and spoken word. Through our limited means, we are simply attempting to help right the centuries' old violence and silencing that should never have occurred in the first place and build alliances and community partnerships with others who share a collective vision for a future far better than today.

INVITATIONS Nomadic Press wholeheartedly accepts invitations to read your work during our open reading period every year. To learn more or to extend an invitation, please visit: www.nomadicpress.org/invitations

DISTRIBUTION
Orders by teachers, libraries, trade bookstores, or wholesalers:

Nomadic Press Distribution
orders@nomadicpress.org
(510) 500-5162

Small Press Distribution
spd@spdbooks.org
(510) 524-1668 / (800) 869-7553

This book was made possible by a loving community of chosen family and friends, old and new.

For author questions or to book a reading at your bookstore, university/school, or alternative establishment, please send an email to info@nomadicpress.org.

Cover art: "Flower of green stone" glyph extrapolated from the image of Huehuecoyotl in the Codex Borbonicus

Published by Nomadic Press, 111 Fairmount Avenue, Oakland, California 94611

First printing, 2022

Library of Congress Cataloging-in-Publication Data
Title: *Chalchiuixochitl / Flor de Piedra Verde / Flower of Jade*
p. cm.
Summary: Las culturas nahua del México antiguo tenían que in xochitl in cuicatl, flor y canto, la poesía, la palabra inspirada era lo único que perduraba porque decía verdad. Chalchiuixochitl/Flor de Piedra Verde/Flower of Jade es un intento de captar las verdades de nuestro tiempo y nuestro mundo a través de una aproximación del lente de la sensibilidad y percepción de nuestros antepasados nahuas. / The Nahua cultures of ancient Mexico held that in xochitl in cuicatl, flor y canto, flower & song, poetry, the inspired word was the only thing that endured because it spoke truth. Chalchiuixochitl/Flor de Piedra Verde/Flower of Jade is an attempt to capture the truths of our time and our world through an approximation of the lens of sensibility and perception of our Nahua forebears.

[1. POETRY / Nahuatl. 2. POETRY / American / Hispanic & Latino. 3. POETRY / Subjects & Themes / Nature. 4. POETRY / Subjects & Themes / Inspirational & Religious. 5. POETRY / American / General.] I. III. Title.

LIBRARY OF CONGRESS CONTROL NUMBER: 2021951151

ISBN: 978-1-955239-26-4

CHALCHIUIXOCHITL
Flor de Piedra Verde
Flower of Jade

poems by RAFAEL JESÚS GONZÁLEZ

CHALCHIUIXOCHITL
Flor de Piedra Verde
Flower of Jade

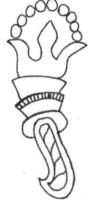

poems by RAFAEL JESÚS GONZÁLEZ

NOMADIC PRESS

a mi padre, madre,
abuelos, abuelas,
hermanos,
ancestros,
hermanos, hermanas
que viven, han vivido, vivirán

tlazocamati

CONTENTS

Cauitl cuicatl: Cantos del tiempo
Cauitl cuicatl: Songs of Time

~

FLOWER OF GREEN STONE: METAPHOR OF NAHUA
POETRY OF PRE-HISPANIC MEXICO

READING GUIDE

INTRODUCCIÓN

Desde niño crecí con flor y canto, poesía que mi padre Jesús Fidel González y mi madre Carmen González Prieto me leían. Me hacían aprender poemas que apenas comprendía para que los recitara en las reuniones familiares cada domingo en casa de mis abuelos maternos 'papanito' Diego González Sosa y mi abuelita Rosario Prieto Gutiérrez. Papanito Diego era de facciones indias y piel morena; abuelita Chayito tenía pelo rojizo, cutis de rosas y crema, facciones criollas. (Mi abuelo paterno Ignacio González había muerto antes de que mis padres se casaran y mi abuela Jovita Ramos presumía de criolla.) Papanito se decía indio (aunque nunca se aclaró de que cultura india); la familia tomaba por supuesto que éramos indio y criollo y de raza nunca se hizo caso. Éramos mexicanos—punto.

Uno de los poemas que más recuerdo es 'México y España' de Juan de Dios Peza. Sospecho que algo tuvo en despertar mi interés por el mundo indígena antes de la llegada de los españoles e impulsó mis estudios en la literatura Nahua. Las fuentes más importantes para mí fueron los *Cantares Mexicanos* (en traducciones al español de Ángel María Garibay K. y Miguel León Portilla) y el *Códice Florentino* (en traducción al inglés de Arthur J.O. Anderson y Charles Dibble.)

De *Los Cantares* los poetas a quienes más les debo son Nezahualcoyotl Señor de Texcoco y Tecayehuatzin Señor de Huexotzino. Del *Códice Florentino* el libro 11, definiciones y descripciones de las cosas terrestres que en si leen como poemas.

Estos me inspiraron a escribir poemas en español/inglés (pues creándome en la frontera estadounidense/mexicana soy bilingüe chicano, chicano desde por allí a mediados de los 1960s. Antes de eso la palabra chicano era sólo argot para mexicano) que recordaran el modo de percibir, de sentir, de pensar, de decir nahua usando la metáfora nahua y sus expresiones.

Espero que en estos poemas se pruebe un cierto sabor, se oiga un eco del antiguo mundo, universo de nuestros antepasados nahuas. Que te sea dulce ese sabor, ameno ese eco.

RAFAEL JESÚS GONZÁLEZ

INTRODUCTION

Since I was a child I grew up with flower & song, poetry that my father Jesús Fidel González and my mother Carmen González Prieto read to me. They had me learn poems that I scarcely understood for me to recite at the family gatherings every Sunday at the home of my maternal grandparents "Papanito" Diego González Sosa and my grandmother Rosario Prieto Gutiérrez.

Papanito Diego had Indian features and dark skin; grandmother Chayito had reddish hair, a complexion of roses and cream, creole features. (My paternal grandfather Ignacio González had died before my parents married, and my grandmother Jovita Ramos presumed to be creole.) Papanito said he was Indian (though of which Indian culture it was never clear); the family took it for a given that we were Indian and creole, and race was never an issue. We were Mexican—period.

One of the poems that I best remember is "Mexico and Spain," by Juan de Dios Peza. I suspect that it had something to do with waking my interest in the indigenous world before the coming of the Spaniards and prompted my studies of Nahua literature. The most important sources for me were the *Cantares Mexicanos* (in Spanish translations by Ángel María Garibay K. and Miguel León Portilla) and the *Florentine Codex* (in English translation by Arthur J.O. Anderson and Charles Dibble).

Of the *Cantares*, the poets to whom I owe the most are Neza-hualcoyotl Lord of Texcoco and Tecayehuatzin Lord of Huexotzino; of the *Florentine Codex*, Book 11, the definitions and descriptions of the Earthly things that in themselves read like poems.

These inspired me to write poems in Spanish and English (being raised on the U.S./Mexican border, I am a bilingual Chicano, Chicano since about the middle 1960s. Before then, the word "chicano" was only slang for Mexican) that would come near the Nahua mode of perceiving, of feeling, of thinking, of saying using Nahua metaphor and its expressions.

I hope that in these poems is tasted a certain flavor, is heard an echo of the ancient world, universe of our Nahua forebears. May that flavor be sweet, that echo pleasing to you.

RAFAEL JESÚS GONZÁLEZ

Poema de Tecayehuatzin Señor de Huexotzinco con versiones en español e inglés de Rafael Jesús González/Poem of Tecayehuatzin Lord of Huexotzinco with versions in Spanish and English by Rafael Jesús González:

Sueño de una palabra/Dream of a Word (c. 1490)

Auh tocnihuane,
tla xoconcaquican in itlatol temictli:
xoxopantla technemitia,
in teocuitlaxilotl, techonythuitia
tlauhquecholetlotl, techoncozcatia.
¡In ticmati ye ontlaneltoca
toyiollo, tocnihuan!

Por favor amigos, oigan ahora
el sueño de una palabra:
en la primavera despertamos
a la borla dorada de la mazorca,
refrigerio la mazorca
y las pruebas de constancia
en los corazones de amigos
nos engalanan el cuello
con collares de joyas.

Please friends, listen now
to the dream of a word:
in spring we wake
to the golden tassel of the maize,
refreshment is the maize,
and the proofs of constancy
in the hearts of friends
about our necks
jeweled collars place.

IN XOCHITL IN CUICATL: FLOR Y CANTO *(arte poético)*

En el Anahuac antiguo se dijo
      que lo más precioso
      lo que más perdura
es la palabra florida.
Sin flor y canto
el corazón duerme
sin sueño de palabra,
amanece sin arcos iris en el cuarto
los cristales fríos y mudos,
las paredes sin ecos de colores.
Si no amamos
      y lo cantamos
si no veneramos
      la vida y la Tierra
corremos peligro;
la primavera será callada, muda
sin el cantar de pájaros,
sorda sin el aleteo de mariposas,
ciega sin el color de las flores.
Amar y cantarlo
      que de nuestro canto
         depende todo.

IN XOCHITL IN CUICATL: FLOWER & SONG (*ars poetica*)

In ancient Anahuac it was said
that what is most precious
what most endures
is the flowering word.
Without flower & song
the heart sleeps
without the dream of a word,
dawns without rainbows in the room,
the crystals cold & mute,
the walls without echoes of color.
If we do not love
        & sing it,
if we do not venerate
        life & the Earth,
we run danger—
Spring will be silent, mute
without the singing of birds,
deaf without the flutter of butterflies,
blind without the color of flowers.
Love & sing it
        for on our song
                all depends.

YOLLOTL: CORAZÓN

La piedra que late es perfecta—
        nada se mide;
se dice: amo; nada importa
        las flores perduran
        aun cuando marchitan;
                el canto es eterno
                el canto vindica
                        el todo
                        la nada
                        el sí
                        el nunca
                        el tal vez.
La mano llama;
        las plumas fragmentan la luz
        y la luz define las plumas.
El caracol es un hueco infinito:
        suena su canto lleno de silencio,
        un eco pleno de copal.
En el rostro se justifica lo posible;
en el corazón se ahoga lo concreto.
        Y allá en el horizonte
                se pierde el encuentro
                se pierde el encuentro
y voltea
                y voltea
                        la luz.

YOLLOTL: HEART

The stone that beats is perfect—
    nothing is measured;
one says: I love; nothing matters
        the flowers last
            even as they wilt;
      song is eternal
      song vindicates
           everything
           nothing
           yes
           never
           perhaps.
The hand calls;
    the plumes fragment the light
    & the light defines the plumes.
The sea-snail is an infinite void:
    it sounds a song full of silence,
    an echo full of copal.
In the face is justified what is possible;
in the heart what is concrete drowns.
    & there in the horizon
      the finding is lost
      the finding is lost
& the light
    turns round
        turns round.

ICNIUHYOTL: LA AMISTAD

Son los amigos
cual aves de rico plumaje
y canto divino
sobre el árbol florido.
    Se ensanchan
    se hacen amplio
        uno al otro
        el corazón.
Sus rostros, sus corazones
son el uno para el otro
    obsidiana clara
    espejos perforados
en que se encuentran
    las flores y el canto
    las plumas más finas
    el oro más puro
    los jades más verdes.
Es en la amistad
que se endiosa el corazón.

ICNIUHYOTL: FRIENDSHIP

Friends are
like birds of rich plumage
& divine song
on the flowering tree.
> They stretch
> they make wide
>> the heart
>> for one another.

Their faces, their hearts
are for each other
> clear obsidian
> perforated mirrors

in which are found
> flowers & song
> the finest feathers
> the purest gold
> the greenest jades.

It is in friendship
that the heart is made god.

CALLI: CASA

Es de espacio labrado
se define el espacio
        gruñe
        canturrea
        canta
        calla.

Nuestros corazones
fugaces como las flores
les envidian raíces:
        en una casa
        pretendemos raíces.

        Decimos:
                en este espacio
                vivimos;
                aquí habita
                nuestro dormir.

Teme la casa que gruña;
        te devorará vivo.
Si no encuentras casa que cante,
        encuentra casa que canturree.
Una casa callada
        se tiene que enseñar a cantar—
            es difícil labor:
        Uno se tiene que ser seguro
        que sea maestro del canto;
        solamente con un corazón de jade
        podremos enseñar
        a nuestros espacios cantar.

CALLI: HOUSE

It is of carved space
space is defined
                    it snarls
                    it hums
                    it sings
                    it is silent.

Our hearts
ephemeral as the flowers
envy them roots;
                    in a house
                    we pretend to roots.
                    We say:
                    in this space we live
                    here our sleeping is housed.

Beware the house that snarls;
                    it will devour you alive.
If you cannot find a house that sings,
                    find one that hums.
A house that is silent
must be taught song—
                    it is a difficult task;
                    one must be certain
                    he is a master of song;
                    only with a heart of jade
                    can we teach our spaces to sing.

ATECOCOLLI: CARACOLA

De la concha del caracol marino
se hace, se pule
      la trompa sagrada.
Se toca, se tañe, se suena.
Con viento de aliento
de aire se hace:
           flores
           plumas
           oro
           jade.
Resuena, llama
      a la reunión,
invoca los cuatro rumbos,
      arriba,
           abajo,
al centro del mundo.
      Resuena, llama,
hace sagrados los espacios.
           Suena la caracola.

ATECOCOLLI: CONCH

Of the conch of the sea snail
is made, is polished
      the sacred trumpet.
It is touched, played, sounded.
With wind of breath
of air are made:
             flowers
             feathers
             gold
             jade.
It resounds, it calls
      to gather,
invokes the four directions,
      above,
             below,
the center of the world.
      It resounds, it calls,
makes spaces sacred.
             The conch sounds.

AYACACHTLI: SONAJA

Es guaje hueco,
       madera cavada;
             contiene guijas
                   del monte
                   del arroyo
                   del mar;
tiene mango
       bien pulido;
             sienta bien a la mano.
Suena cuando se agita,
             suena,
suena como la culebra cascabel.
       La mano le presta ritmo:
            suena alegre
                 suena lúgubre;
       incita a los pies.
Es cetro de Xochipilli,
       es instrumento del músico,
             instrumento del danzante:
       incita a los pies a bailar.

AYACACHTLI: RATTLE

It is a hollow gourd,
        hollow wood;
                it contains pebbles
                        from the mountain
                        from the creek
                        from the sea;
it has a handle
        well polished;
                it suits the hand well.
It sounds when shaken,
                        it sounds,
it sounds like the rattlesnake.
            The hand gives it rhythm:
                it sounds joyful
                        it sounds mournful;
            it incites the feet.
It is Xochipilli's scepter,
            it is instrument of the musician,
                    instrument of the dancer:
            it incites the feet to dance.

TLATOLLI TLACOTL: BASTÓN DE LA PALABRA

Tomando en mano este palo, vara, bastón
  tienes la palabra—
que sea alumbrada por la luz del sol,
llena de la sabiduría de la serpiente,
la verdad, la belleza de flor y canto.
Que sea atestiguada por la Tierra,
que sea para el sanar.
Que sean tus palabras, tu decir
  guirnalda de flores
  tejido de plumas
  pendientes de oro
  collar de jade.
Oigamos tu verdad,
conozcamos tu rostro, tu corazón.

TLATOLLI TLACOTL: TALKING STICK

Taking in hand this stick, wand, baton
       you have the word —
may it be lit by the light of the sun,
filled with the wisdom of the serpent,
the truth, the beauty of flower & song.
Let it be witnessed by the Earth,
let it be for the healing.
May your words, your telling be
       garland of flowers
       weaving of feathers
       earrings of gold
       necklace of jade.
Let us hear your truth;
know your face, your heart.

TEOCUITLATOMIN: MONEDA

Tiene brillo
no tiene brillo;
vale
vale una joya
     una pluma
     una flor
una canción.

TEOCUITLATOMIN: COIN

It is bright
it is dull;
it has value
it is worth a jewel
          a feather
          a flower
a song.

CENTLI: MAÍZ

El maíz dicen los abuelos, las abuelas
brota en flor modesta y humilde,
luego su borla roja, penacho de plumas,
en su madurez la mazorca
es de granos de oro, cuentas de piedra verde.
Pulsera, decían, preciosa,
nuestra carne, nuestros huesos.

Sabían los ancianos, ancianas;
lo sabemos nosotros
ahora cuando brujos de mala fe,
de visión equivocada
impulsados por la codicia
envenenan la semilla sagrada
con esencia de alacrán
y hacen yerma la milpa.

Despertemos, sublevémonos
hijos, hijas del maíz—
basta de brujos y embusteros—
es nuestra vida que defendemos,
nuestro sustento, nuestro santo maíz.

CENTLI: CORN

Corn, say the grandfathers, grandmothers
blooms in a modest, humble flower,
then its red tassel, headdress of feathers,
in its ripeness the corn cob
is of grains of gold, beads of green stone.
Bracelet, they said, precious,
        our flesh, our bones.

The ancients knew it;
we know it
when sorcerers of bad faith,
        of mistaken vision
driven by greed
poison the sacred seed
with the essence of scorpion
& make waste the corn field.

Let us awake, let us rebel,
sons, daughters of the corn—
enough of sorcerers & cheats—
it is our lives that we defend,
our sustenance, our holy corn.

LAS TRES HERMANAS

Son tres hermanas—
dicen los abuelos, las abuelas—
    El maíz, el frijol, la calabaza—
    vienen de los dioses, las diosas
cuentan y muchas son sus historias.
Se aman unas a las otros;
conviven lozanas y alegres
con nuestro cuidado, nuestra atención
como se merecen, como es debido—
vienen de los dioses, las diosas.
Son nuestro alimento, nuestro sostén.
Son la vida, don de la Tierra.

THE THREE SISTERS

They are three sisters,
say the grandfathers, the grandmothers—
        the corn, the bean, the squash—
they come from the gods, the goddesses
they tell & many are their stories
They love one another;
They live together healthy & happy
with our care, our attention
as they merit, as is right—
they come from the gods, the goddesses.
They are our food, our sustenance.
They are life, gift of the Earth.

CHIMALXOCHITL: MIRASOL

Flor escudo se le llama,
Semeja, mira al sol;
Es redonda, sus pétalos
como rayos de sol.
Flor escudo del Señor
Colibrí-del-Sur.
Obsequio del comerciante
viajero, embajador,
a las personas distinguidas.
Sus semillas en espiral,
abundantes, sabrosas;
medicinales dicen.
Chimalxochitl, mirasol.

CHIMALXOCHITL: SUNFLOWER

Shield Flower it is called,
It looks like, gazes at the sun;
It is round, its petals
like the rays of the sun.
Shield flower of Lord
Hummingbird-of-the-South.
Gift of the traveling
merchant, ambassador,
to distinguished persons.
Its seeds in a spiral,
abundant, tasty;
medicinal they say.
Chimalxochitl, sunflower.

NOPALLI: NOPAL

Crece en pencas
como tantas orejas de jade
verdes, tiernas, sabrosas
aun llenas de espinas.
Sus flores como escudos
de plumas doradas.
Su fruto como corazones
rojos, tiernos, dulces
tal vez porque escuchan
los cantos de las aves,
estas tantas orejas de jade.

NOPALLI: PRICKLY-PEAR

It grows in paddles
like so many ears of jade,
green, tender, tasty
though full of thorns.
Its flowers like shields
of golden feathers.
Its fruit like hearts
red, tender, sweet
perhaps because they listen
to the birds' songs,
these many ears of jade.

OCELOTL: JAGUAR

Es Ocelotl
   es Balam
es el Señor Jaguar,
    rey de la jungla.
Se dice que las brasas
   de la fogata
en que se hizo el sol
le marcaron la piel.
  Su rugir es terrible,
   sus ojos espejos dorados,
sus garras, sus colmillos—terribles.
Es el sol nocturno—
   vaga por la noche,
   la oscuridad es su reino.
Es el corazón del monte,
octavo guardián de la noche.

OCELOTL: JAGUAR

It is Ocelotl
        it is Balam
it is the Lord Jaguar,
      king of the jungle.
It is said that the embers
      of the blaze
in which the sun was made
left their marks on his skin.
      His roar is terrible,
      his eyes are gold mirrors,
his claws, his fangs—terrible.
He is the nocturnal sun—
    he roams the night,
      the darkness is his realm.
He is the heart of the mountain,
the eighth guardian of the night.

OZOMATLI: EL MONO

Es el sagaz, el sensual,
guardián del onceno día
del almanaque de los destinos,
    afortunado y feliz;
el comerciante, el embajador
    lleva su mano
como talismán de la suerte.

Lo estima el viento,
lo ama el Príncipe de las Flores;
con él baila, se deleita.
Suya es la gente del segundo sol.

Se dice que inventó el escribir,
el bailar—suya es la quinta copa;
no cree que haya exceso del goce.

Tiene manos, pies, cabeza sagaz,
cola; es ágil, inquieto, travieso.
Su voz no es para flor y canto,
sin embargo acompaña
al Señor de las Flores.
Es listo, sensual.
No conforme con lo bastante
quiere a lo menos una flor más.
No distingue entre la pluma y el oro.
Busca el jade en el exceso del goce,
nagual del Príncipe de las flores.

OZOMATLI: THE MONKEY

He is the clever one, the sensual,
guardian of the eleventh day
of the almanac of destinies,
        blessed & happy;
the merchant, the ambassador
        carries his hand
as token of luck.

The wind esteems him,
the Prince of Flowers loves him;
he dances with him, delights.
His are the people of the second sun.

It is said he invented writing,
dancing—his is the fifth cup;
he does not believe there is excess of joy.

He has hands, feet, a clever head,
a tail; he is agile, restless, mischievous.
His voice is not for flower & song,
nevertheless he accompanies
the Lord of Flowers.
He is clever, sensual.
Not content with enough
he wants at least one more flower.
He does not distinguish
        between feather & gold.
He seeks jade in the excess of joy,
familiar of the Prince of Flowers.

MIZTLI: PUMA

Es cuguar, puma, pantera, león montés;
habita en los montes, entre los pinos,
el mezquite, la artemisia, los nopales.
Hace su lecho en las peñas del cerro,
 en las cuevas de las lomas.
Caza a los animales del bosque,
  del campo, a los venados.
 Es temible su rugir—
   sus garras, sus colmillos.
Varía su color: pardo, rojizo,
color palomilla, color piloncillo.
 Como el sol del desierto
  es hermoso, feroz.

MIZTLI: COUGAR

He is cougar, puma, panther, mountain lion;
he lives in the mountains, among the pines,
the mesquite, the sage, the prickly-pears.
He makes his bed on the mountain stones.
      in the caves of the hills.
He hunts the animals of the wood,
          the fields, the deer.
      Fearful is his roar—
          his claws, his fangs.
His color varies: brown, reddish,
palomino colored, color of brown sugar.
      Like the sun of the desert
          he is beautiful, fierce.

AYOTOCHTLI: ARMADILLO

Es criatura nocturna
vaga bajo la luz
de la luna, las estrellas—
   es apacible
se alimenta de hormigas.
Se protege con armadura
   de hueso, de cuerno.
El que habita la tierra de Aztlan
lleva las nueve bandas
de los guardianes de la noche.
   Es apacible y callado.

AYOTOCHTLI: ARMADILLO

He is a nocturnal creature,
he wanders under the light
of the moon, the stars—
       he is peaceable,
feeds on ants.
He protects himself with armor
       of bone, of horn.
He who dwells in the land of Aztlan
wears the nine bands
of the guardians of the night.
       He is peaceable & quiet.

TLACUATZIN: ZARIGÜEYA

Se dice que la chispa
de una estrella
encendió los bosques
y los guardianes terrestres
se apoderaron del fuego
defendiéndolo con un jaguar feróz
pero el tlacuache sufriendo frío
con la cola se robó una brasa
y llevándola en su bolsa
nos trajo el fuego.
Es por eso que el tlacuache
no tiene pelo en la cola.

TLACUATZIN: OPOSSUM

It is said that a spark
from a star
set the forests on fire
and the Earth guardians
took possession of fire
protecting it with a fierce jaguar
but opossum suffering cold
with his tail stole an ember
and carrying it in her pouch
brought us fire.
That is why the opossum
has no hair on its tail.

PAPALOTL: MARIPOSA

Gran y venerable mariposa,
flor en vuelo,
      en movimiento,
alas como si pintadas por tolteca,
    hija del sol,
señora de la lumbre y del alma
se alimenta del néctar
      de la flor y del canto;
es transformación su vida
      breve y fugaz.

PAPALOTL: BUTTERFLY

Great & venerable butterfly,
flower in flight,
  in movement,
wings as if painted by a Toltec,
  daughter of the sun,
lady of fire & of the soul,
she feeds on the nectar
  of flower & song;
transformation is her life
  brief & fleeting.

XOCHIOLLIN: MOVIMIENTO FLORIDO

El movimiento florido
es la danza del Príncipe de las Flores
   del Señor Cinco Flor
que lleva en el corazón
  su flor de cinco pétalos;
    de allí el canto florido.
Su exceso es en amar,
lo busca en medicina sagrada,
se deleita en la flor y la pluma,
de oro se forma el rostro,
  de jade el corazón.
Se viste del arco iris
y alrededor del árbol de la vida
es su bailar, movimiento florido.

XOCHIOLLIN: FLOWERING MOVEMENT

Flowering movement is
the dance of the Prince of Flowers
        of Lord Five Flower
who carries in the heart
    his flower of five petals;
        from there is flowering song.
His excess is in loving,
he seeks it in the sacred medicine,
he delights in flower & feather,
of gold he molds his face,
        of jade his heart.
He dresses in the rainbow
& around the tree of life
his dance, flowering movement.

CHALCHIUHYOLLOTL: CORAZÓN DE PIEDRA VERDE

Es de piedra verde—
      hace del rostro
      espejo perforado,
rompe las máscaras,
      se forma el rostro.
Es serpiente, es ave
      es cristal, es prisma:
quiebra la luz y la colora
la vuelve a hacer clara
      es como el agua.
Canta: es silencio sin alas
baila: es quietud sin peso
      vuela, vuela y calla.
      Arregla flores
      teje plumas
      funde oro
      se labra de jade
nombra las cosas, las endiosa
      se endiosa a sí mismo,
taja el caracol marino,
con él se adorna el pecho
      y se corona de estrellas
      y obsidiana.
Se abre y endiosa a lo que entra
por su espacio amplio y estrecho.
      Enciende copal
      bendice y alaba
      nombra
      nombra y calla.

CHALCHIUHYOLLOTL: HEART OF GREEN STONE

It is of green stone—
    it makes a perforated mirror
      of the face,
it shatters masks,
  it forms a face.
     It is serpent, it is bird
        it is crystal, a prism:
it breaks the light & colors it
makes it clear again
     it is like water.
It sings: silence without wings
it dances: stillness without weight
    it flies, flies & is still.
          It arranges flowers
         weaves feathers
         casts gold
         carves itself of jade
it names things, deifies them
    makes itself god,
cuts the shell of the sea snail,
with it adorns the breast
      & crowns itself with stars
       & with obsidian.
It opens & deifies what enters
through its space narrow & wide.
    It burns copal
      blesses & gives praise
     names
       names & is still.

40

CANTO A MIS HERMANOS

Hermano—
se erige florido el árbol de la vida
en que cantan las aves.

Hermano—
              venimos de la misma madre
                        del mismo padre—
no sé si habitamos el mismo mundo.

Hermano, hay cariño, hay ternura
he querido hablarte desde muy hondo;
              entre nuestros rostros
                        nuestros corazones
              hay telarañas de silencio.
Nuestras dichas
nuestras penas
nos son extrañas uno al otro.
              Probamos distintas flores
                        distintas espinas—
nos es difícil describir
              sus formas, sus colores.

Quisiera darte
          o pedirte
          la mano,
darte aliento, consuelo—
          quisiera tocarte, hermano.

SONG TO MY BROTHERS

Brother—
the flowering tree of life
in which the birds sing rises.

Brother—
       we come from the same mother
                from the same father—
I do not know if we inhabit the same world.

Brother, there is love, there is tenderness;
I have wanted to speak to you from very deep;
       between our faces
              our hearts
     there are cobwebs of silence.
Our joys
our griefs
are strange to one another.
      We taste different flowers
             different thorns—
it is hard for us to describe
       their forms, their colors.

I want to give you
      or ask for
        a hand,
give you breath, comfort—
        I want to touch you, brother.

CANTO PARA EL ENCUENTRO DE UN AMIGO

Amigo—
        tus ojos son espejos perforados;
        en ellos me veo yo y el más allá—
            (tu corazón contiene
                flores
                plumas
                pedazos de jade)
      Tu voz está llena
          del olor de flores
          del sonido del canto.
     En tus pies está el polvo
          de caminos por la oscuridad
          de caminos hacia la luz.

     Hemos caminado largas distancias;
     nuestras manos han anhelado tocarse.

Te reconozco:
tu cara, tu corazón.

Hermano:
        por lo que ha sido
                gracias
        por lo que es
                albricias
        por lo que será
43   sí.

SONG FOR MEETING A FRIEND

Friend—
       your eyes are perforated mirrors;
       in them I see myself & beyond—
           (Your heart holds
               flowers
               feathers
               pieces of jade)
    Your voice is full
          of the smell of flowers
          of the sound of song.
    On your feet is the dust
          of paths leading thru darkness
          of paths leading to light.

    We have traveled long distances;
    our hands have longed to touch.

I recognize you:
your face, your heart.

Brother:
       for what has been
               thanks
          for what is
             joy
          for what will be
            yes.

NEMICTILIZTLI CUICATL: CANCIÓN PARA BODA

Ante nuestro, nuestra
>> Señor-Señora de la Dualidad
vienen a lomo de las abuelas
>> de los abuelos:
>> cambien flores
>> cambien cantos.

Sean gozosos—
>> sus rostros
>> sus corazones
>> voltean uno hacia al otro:
>> crecerán flores
>> tejerán plumas
>> ensartarán cuentas de jade.

Alégrense:
>> el vino es fragante
>> el pan es dulce.

Sus mantos se amarran
>> uno con el otro;
el lazo de flores
ciñe sus hombros, une sus vidas.

Escuchen este canto de bendición;
>> los dioses sonríen y bailan.
>> Alégrense:
>> el vino es fragante
>> el pan es dulce.

NEMICTILIZTLI CUICATL: SONG FOR A WEDDING

Before Our Lord-Our Lady of Duality
you come on the backs of grandmothers
                        of grandfathers:
            exchange flowers
            exchange songs.

Be joyful—
            your faces
            your hearts
            turn each to the other:
            they will grow flowers
                        weave feathers
                            string beads of jade.

            Rejoice:
                        the wine is fragrant
                        the bread is sweet.

Your cloaks are tied
            each to the other;
the rope of flowers
rings your shoulders, yokes your lives.

Hear this song of blessing;
            the gods smile & dance.
                        Rejoice:
                                the wine is fragrant
                                the bread is sweet.

PARA EL BAUTIZO DE UN PROFETA

Con este rito
          se te da nombre
          se te llama
          se te advierte:
aquí heredas los mitos
formarás máscaras
te harás dueño de la tinta negra
                    la tinta roja.
Probarás las espinas del maguey
          las flores
          las confundirás
          se te mezclarán en la sangre
          engendrarán cantos.
En observatorios de turquesa
estudiarás soles vivos, soles muertos;
          tendrás que distinguir
          los unos de los otros.
Sólo así te harás dueño de un corazón
                    de un rostro;
          sólo así se endiosa el corazón
                    se labra de jade
                    se pule con obsidiana.
          Fundirás tus máscaras
                    para formarte el rostro.
Llegará el tiempo
          en que tajes el caracol marino;

FOR THE BAPTISM OF
A PROPHET

With this rite
  you are named
  you are called
  you are advised:
here you inherit the myths
you will form masks
you will become master of the black ink
                    the red ink.
You will taste the thorns of the cactus
        the flowers;
        you will confuse them
        they will mix in your blood
        they will engender songs.
In observatories of turquoise
you will study live suns, dead suns;
        you will have to distinguish
        one from the other.
Only thus will you become master of a heart
                        of a face;
        only thus is the heart made god
                is carved from jade
                is polished with obsidian.
        You will smelt your masks
                to form your face.
The time will come
        in which you will cut the sea-snail;

con él te adornarás el pecho.

Entonces
    bajo las máscaras de los dioses
        las máscaras de obsidiana
    encontrarás el Sí;
        sus definiciones son infinitas.

With it you will adorn your breast.

Then,

      under the masks of the gods
          the masks of obsidian
    you will find the Yes;
         its definitions are infinite.

PARA LA INICIACIÓN DE UN MAESTRO

Adórnate el pecho con el caracol marino,
　　　dueño de las palabras sacras,
　　　sacerdote de la luna de obsidiana clara.
La estrella vespertina dará luz a tus sueños;
el águila glorificará tu camino.

　　　Mira, amigo;
　　　　　te doy flores encarnadas
　　　　　como el licor sagrado;
　　　　　canto, como el murmurar del mar.
Labrarás de jade el corazón,
tomarás posesión de la tinta roja, la tinta negra,
enriquecerás a la gente
　　　se formarán rostros.

Adórnate el pecho con el caracol marino:
　　　entra al teocalli, casa divina;
　　　ensaya los cantos; toma asiento;
　　　toma ablución; toma el manto blanco,
　　　el maíz, las flores;
　　　enciende el copal, el fuego;
　　　desparrama agua; ofrece frutos.
Tu amigo te ensarta un collar de flores
　　　　　　　de canto—
Alégrate—
　　　sé alabado:
Adórnate el pecho con el caracol marino.

FOR THE INITIATION OF A TEACHER

Adorn your breast with the sea-snail,
      master of the sacred words,
        priest of the clear obsidian moon.
The evening star will light your dreams,
the eagle will glorify your path.

      Look, friend:
              I give you red flowers
              like the sacred liquor,
                song like the murmur of the sea.
You shall carve your heart of jade,
possess the red ink, the black ink,
scatter precious plumes,
enrich the people—
      they shall form a face.

Adorn your breast with the sea-snail:
      Enter the divine house;
      practice the songs, be seated,
      take ablution, take the white cloth,
      the corn, the flowers,
      light incense, fire,
      scatter water, offer fruit.

Your friend strings you a collar of flowers
                  of song—
Be joyful—
            be praised:
Adorn your breast with the sea-snail.

TEIXCUITIANI: MAESTRO
al Prof. Dr. John Sharp

Maestro de cuatrocientas lenguas
     domó mil voces,
recogió guirnaldas de flores y cantos,
      dio forma a los rostros,
         alumbró los corazones.
Dueño de la tinta negra, la tinta roja
compartió lo que sabía
        collares, pulseras de oro;
     adornó el saber de otros.
Por el estudio
     con la enseñanza
se labró de jade el corazón,
        se lo endiosó.
Maestro de maestros
dejó un tesoro de ecos,
      pabellones de plumas ricas,
para indicar el camino
       al reino de los dioses.

TEIXCUITIANI: TEACHER
al Prof. Dr. John Sharp

Master of four-hundred tongues,
        he mastered a myriad voices,
gathered garlands of flowers & songs,
        gave form to faces
                & illumined hearts.
Master of the black ink, the red ink,
he shared what he knew,
                collars, bracelets of gold,
        & adorned the knowing of others.
Through study
        through teaching
he carved his heart of jade,
                deified it.
Teacher of teachers,
he left a treasure of echoes,
        flags of rich plumes,
to mark the way
                to the realm of the gods.

LOS PÉTALOS DE XOCHIPILLI

El movimiento de la vida
y el capricho de los vientos
esparcen los pétalos
de la flor del príncipe
pero siempre serán suyos;
siempre la flor y el canto,
la hermandad de la visión y el arte.
Los llaman la concha y la flauta,
el tambor y la sonaja—
su movimiento es la danza.
Separados por la distancia y el tiempo
los une el corazón florido del príncipe
que ni de distancia ni de tiempo conoce.

THE PETALS OF XOCHIPILLI

The movement of life
& the whim of the winds
scatter the petals
of the prince's flower,
but they will always be his;
always flower & song,
the brotherhood of vision & art.
The conch & the flute,
the drum & the rattle call them—
their movement is the dance.
Separated by distance & time
they are linked by the prince's flowering heart
that knows of neither distance nor time

YOLIZTLI: LA VIDA
(sobre lo que dijo Nezahualcoyotl)

La vida es —dijo el viejo rey—
    una luciérnaga en la noche.
        La muerte marchita las flores
        desgarra las plumas finas
        desmorona el oro
        quiebra el jade.

Un día,
    despojados hasta los huesos,
            nos iremos,
la única cosa digna de tener,
como hicimos dios al corazón:
        las canciones que cantamos
        los bailes que bailamos
        los seres que amamos.

YOLIZTLI: LIFE
(on what Nezahualcoyotl said)

Life is, said the old king,
     a firefly in the night.
          Death wilts the flowers
          tears the fine feathers
          crumbles the gold
          shatters the jade.

One day,
     stripped to the bones,
               we go,
the only thing worth the having,
how we made the heart god:
          the songs we sang
          the dances we danced
          the ones we loved.

PÉTALOS DE CEMPOALXOCHITL

Pétalos de cempoal
riegan el camino hacia Mictlan
    tierra incógnita.

Sólo conocemos el camino:
    flores marchitas
    plumas rotas
    oro en polvo
    piedras verdes en añicos.

De vez en cuando
    una flor cabal
        el eco de un canto.

PETALS OF MARIGOLD

Petals of marigolds
sprinkle the way to Mictlan,
            unknown land.

We know only the way:
            wilted flowers
            torn feathers
            gold dust
            crumbled green stones.

From time to time
            a whole flower
                        the echo of a song.

CONSEJO PARA EL PEREGRINO A MICTLAN

Cruza el campo amarillo de cempoales,
baja al reino de las sombras;
                            es amplio, es estrecho.
Interroga a los ancianos;
                        son sabios, son necios:

        —Señores míos, Señoras mías,
    ¿Qué verdad dicen sus flores, sus cantos?
    ¿Son verdaderamente bellas, ricas sus plumas?
    ¿No es el oro sólo excremento de los dioses?
    Sus jades, ¿son los más finos, los más verdes?
    Su legado, ¿es tinta negra, tinta roja?—

            Acepta sólo lo preciso:

lo que te haga amplio el corazón
lo que te ilumine el rostro.

ADVICE FOR THE PILGRIM TO MICTLAN

Cross the yellow fields of marigolds,
descend to the realm of shadows;
                        it is wide, it is narrow.
Question the ancients;
                    they are wise, they are fools:

      "My Lords, My Ladies,
What truth do your flowers, your songs tell?
Are your feathers truly lovely, truly rich?
Is not gold only the excrement of the gods?
Your jades, are they the finest, the most green?
Your legacy, is it black ink, red ink? "

      Accept only the necessary:

what will widen your heart
what will enlighten your face.

PARA SACERDOTES DE XOCHIPILLI DIFUNTOS
a Roberto Almanzán y Juan Domingo

La vida es rica y breve
como arco iris que mide
de un punto del tiempo a otro
y esfumándose como humo de copal
deja vacías las manos
de Xochipilli, Príncipe de las flores,
perdidas sus flores y sus sonajas.

FOR DECEASED PRIESTS OF XOCHIPILLI
to Roberto Almanzán & Juan Domingo

Life is rich & brief
like a rainbow that measures
from a point in time to another
& fading like incense smoke
leaves empty the hands
of Xochipilli, Prince of flowers,
lost his flowers & his rattles.

IHIYOTL: ALIENTO

Con la lengua se teje el aliento;
hacemos flores de canto.
Decimos:
>   Esto perdura
>   aun cuando
>   se esfuma la vida.

Es ilusión;
los tejidos se deshilachan,
los libros se pudren, se queman,
los puntitos de luz se apagan
y de nuestras vidas
ni los luceros
se acuerdan.

IHIYOTL: BREATH

Breath is woven with the tongue;
we make flowers of song.
We say:
> This lasts
> even when
> life goes.
It is illusion;
the weavings unravel,
the books rot, burn,
the little points of light go out,
& of our lives
not even the stars
remember.

UN SACERDOTE DESTERRADO SE DIRIGE A COATLICUE

Ave, Madre cabeza de serpiente,
      Madre faldas de serpiente—

Los estambres se han formado
en pájaros volantes cagando flores,
      el amate se ha machacado
      las tintas se han untado
      para formar pájaros desposados
      vistos sólo en sueños.
Las flores y cantos se han tejido;
no se han creído las tintas rojas, las tintas negras.

      Madre collar de manos y corazones—

Somos planetas;
conversamos con nuestros corazones;
somos dueños de un rostro, un corazón,
pero entre nosotros son grandes las distancias.
      Una vez hubo grandes árboles
      y las aguas le hablaban fuertemente
      al gavilán escuchante.
La crueldad conocía el color, el olor de la sangre.

AN EXILED PRIEST ADDRESSES COATLICUE

Ave, serpent-headed Mother
      serpent-skirted Mother—

The yarns have been shaped
to flying birds that shit flowers,
      the amate paper pounded
      & the paints spread
      to form mating birds
      seen only in dreams.
The flowers & song have been woven;
the red & the black inks have not been believed.

      Mother collared in hearts & hands—

We are planets;
we converse with our hearts;
we are masters of a face & a heart,
but the distances are great among us.
      Once there were great trees
      & the waters spoke loudly
      to the listening hawks.
Cruelty knew the heat & color of blood.

Madre cinturón de culebra,
       hebilla de calavera—
Los mares han sido violados
y las aves marinas ennegrecidas
reclaman a la luna violada.

       Madre manos de serpiente,
       Madre pies de águila—

Tu hijo te ha traicionado
y los trece cielos
que cargas a cuestas
los ha envenenado.
La obsidiana con que nos cortamos las manos
labrando instrumentos de sacrificio
está abandonada.
Ya no es sagrado el dolor
y por lo que pagamos con nuestra sangre
ya no es la vida.

Snake-belted,
skull-buckled Mother—
The seas are defiled
& the blackened sea birds
cry to the defiled moon.

      Serpent-handed,
      Eagle-footed Mother—

Your son has betrayed you
& the thirteen heavens
you carry on your back
have been poisoned.
The obsidian we cut our hands on
shaping tools of sacrifice
is abandoned.
Pain is no longer sacred
& what we pay for with our blood
is no longer life.

CANTO CHUECO DE QUILTICOYOTZIN

Hay veces que la flor y canto
que Quilticoyotzin alza
a la luna, le sale chueco;
le pesa el corazón—
secas las flores,
las plumas sin color,
sin lustre el oro,
desparramados los jades.
Se marchita la flor
se retuerce el canto
la luna se esconde
tras el nopal.

QUILTICOYOTZIN'S CROOKED SONG

There are times when the flower & song
Quilticoyotzin raises
to the moon comes out crooked;
his heart is heavy—
dried the flowers,
the feathers without color,
without luster the gold,
scattered the jades.
      The flower wilts
      the song twists
      the moon hides
      behind the prickly-pear.

FLOR Y CANTO PARA NUESTROS TIEMPOS

La flor y canto que nos llega
es desarraigado—
    se marchitan la flores,
        se desgarran las plumas,
        se desmorona el oro,
            se quiebra el jade.
No importa que tan denso el humo de copal,
    cuantos los corazones ofrendados,
se desarraigan los mitos,
    mueren los dioses.
Tratamos de salvarlos
de las aguas oscuras del pasado
con anzuelos frágiles
forjados de imaginación y anhelo.
Dentro llevamos voces mixtas—
abuelas, abuelos
conquistados y conquistadores
    —nuestro legado.
De él tenemos que escoger lo preciso,
    lo negro, lo rojo,
cultivar nuestras propias flores,
cantar nuestros propios cantos,
recoger plumas nuevas para adornarnos,
oro para formarnos el rostro,
buscar jade para labrarnos el corazón—
sólo así crearemos el nuevo mundo.

FLOWER & SONG FOR OUR TIMES

The flower & Song that comes to us
is uprooted—
    flowers wither,
       feathers tear,
          gold crumbles,
             jade breaks.
It matters not how thick the incense smoke,
   how many the hearts offered,
myths are uprooted,
   the gods die.
We try to save them
from the dark waters of the past
with fragile hooks
forged of imagination & longing.
Within we carry mixed voices—
grandmothers, grandfathers
conquered & conquerors
   —our legacy.
From it we have to choose the necessary,
   the black & the red,
grow our own flowers,
sing our own songs,
gather new feathers to adorn ourselves,
discover new gold to form our face,
seek jade to carve our hearts—
only thus can we create the new world.

REZO A HUEHUECOYOTL

Señor Coyote Viejo,
     Señor del regocijo de la carne,
levanta tu flor de jade,
       tu sonaja de oro;
luce tu penacho de plumas,
       tu manto bordado;
a la luna levanta la quinta copa.
Señor del canto, Señor de la danza,
     Señor del deleite sensual,
sálvanos de la prudencia cobarde,
      máscara opresiva
que pretende ponerle buena cara
     a la cobardía prudente.
Señor del exceso,
        Señor del festín,
deslúmbranos con la vida.

PRAYER TO HUEHUECOYOTL

Old Lord Coyote,
      Lord of the flesh's rejoicing,
raise your flower of jade,
        your rattle of gold;
sport your headdress of plumes,
        your embroidered cape;
raise high the fifth cup to the moon.
Lord of the song, Lord of the dance,
      Lord of sensual delight,
save us from cowardly prudence,
        oppressive mask
that pretends to put a good face
        on prudent cowardliness.
Lord of the feast,
           Lord of excess,
        overwhelm us with life.

REZO A XOCHIPILLI

Niño, noble, príncipe de las flores,
señor de la visión y del soñar,
de la flor y canto que con las artes
abres el corazón y lo deleitas,
señor de la vida impaciente
con límites arbitrarios
alza la quinta copa
y embriaga al sobrio;
señor de los juegos espanta
al tímido, al temeroso
con tu movimiento florido;
escandaliza con arcos iris
a los quienes vieran
el mundo en blanco y negro.
Señor de la vida y el exceso,
señor del arte: flor la palabra,
pluma el sueño, oro la visión,
piedra verde el corazón—
              Príncipe de las Flores.

PRAYER TO XOCHIPILLI

Child, noble, prince of flowers,
lord of vision & of dreaming,
of flower & song who with the arts
opens the heart & delights it,
lord of life impatient
with arbitrary limits
raise the fifth cup
& intoxicate the sober.
Lord of games, startle
the timid, the fearful
with your flowering movement;
scandalize with rainbows
those who would see
the world in black & white.
Lord of life & of excess,
lord of art: flower the word,
feather the dream, gold the vision,
green stone the heart—
          Prince of Flowers.

XOCHIPILLI, XOCHIQUETZAL

Xochipilli, Príncipe de las flores,
Xochiquetzal, Flor preciosa,
dios, diosa del arte, del amor
su flor de cinco pétalos
perfuma el corazón—
la poesía, la música, la danza,
todas las artes son su dominio;
luz, canto del corazón,
corona de plumas y oro,
joyas de piedra verde
engalanan el corazón.

XOCHIPILLI, XOCHIQUETZAL

Xochipilli, Prince of Flowers,
Xochiquetzal, Precious Blossom,
god, goddess of art, of love
your flower of five petals
perfumes the heart—
poetry, music, dance,
all the arts are your dominion;
light, song of the heart,
crown of feathers & gold,
jewels of greenstone
adorn the heart.

REZO A TONANTZIN

Tonantzin
    madre de todo
    lo que de ti vive,
es, habita, mora, está;
Madre de todos los dioses
             las diosas
madre de todos nosotros,
    la nube y el mar
    la arena y el monte
    el musgo y el árbol
    el ácaro y la ballena.

Derramando flores
haz de mi manto un recuerdo
que jamás olvidemos que tú eres
único paraíso de nuestro vivir.

Bendita eres,
cuna de la vida, fosa de la muerte,
fuente del deleite, piedra del sufrir.

concédenos, madre, justicia,
    concédenos, madre, la paz.

PRAYER TO TONANTZIN

Tonantzin
      mother of all
      that of you lives,
be, dwells, inhabits, is;
Mother of all the gods
          the goddesses
Mother of us all,
      the cloud & the sea
      the sand & the mountain
      the moss & the tree
      the mite & the whale.

Spilling flowers
make of my cloak a reminder
that we never forget that you are
the only paradise of our living.

Blessed are you,
cradle of life, grave of death,
fount of delight, rock of pain.

Grant us, mother, justice,
      grant us, mother, peace.

NUESTRO MOVIMIENTO, NUESTRA REVOLUCIÓN

Es nuestro movimiento,
        nuestra revolución
de corazón y consciencia;
es por la Tierra, la justicia, la paz.
Amar y regocijo son nuestras armas,
flor y canto. La hacemos
con corazón y rostro,
con lo que tenemos de oro,
plumas, piedra verde.
Es para el sanar—
        nuestro movimiento,
        nuestra revolución.

OUR MOVEMENT, OUR REVOLUTION

Our movement,
          our revolution is
of the heart & consciousness;
It is for the Earth, justice, peace;
Loving and joy are our weapons,
flower & song. We make it
with heart and face
with what we have of gold,
feathers, green stone.
It is for the healing—
          our movement,
                    our revolution.

CAUITL CUICATL:
CANTOS DEL TIEMPO

CAUITL CUICATL:
SONGS OF TIME

1 TLANTEYOTIA: APRECIO

Llega un tiempo,
     un punto,
          una altura,
si no de sabiduría,
     de años,
cuando uno llama a sí
sus bienes,
el oro, las plumas finas.

Dice: Esto he logrado;
en esto, mi inversión;
        esto me hace rico.
Como el viejo rey
Coyote-Que-Hambrea,
dice: Soy rico;
soy conocedor de jades
son mis amig@s.

1 TLANTEYOTIA: APPRAISAL

A time comes,
      a point,
            a height,
if not of wisdom,
      of years,
when one calls in
his wealth,
the gold, the fine feathers.

He says: This I have accomplished;
      in this, my investment;
            this makes me rich.
Like the old king
Coyote-Who-Hungers,
he says: I am rich;
I am a knower of jades—
            they are my friends.

2 POUALI: CUENTA

Cuando se atan, se anudan los años,
cuando uno llama a sí
      sus bienes,
el oro, las plumas finas.
los más verdes de sus jades,

se avalora todo —

      las piedras más mezquinas,
        las hojas,
          los momentos —

Todo modela el rostro
         forma el corazón —
   lo claro,
      lo oscuro.

Se reconocen los jades más finos —
   son los seres queridos.

Se sabe:
   es necia la cabeza;
   es sabio el corazón.

2 POUALI: ACCOUNT

When the years are tied, knotted,
when one calls in
          his wealth,
the gold, the fine feathers,
the most green of his jades,

everything is valued—

          the smallest stones,
                    the leaves,
                              the moments—

everything shapes the face,
                              forms the heart—
the light,
          the dark.

One recognizes the finest jades—
          they are those we love.

One knows:
          the head is foolish;
          the heart is wise.

3 TOLTECUEUETIA: EL ARTE DEL ENVEJECER

Se dice que el envejecer es un arte—
los momentos que dan forma a los años
        se componen, se tejen,
        se moldean, se labran.
Se componen de flor y canto,
        y de espina y llanto;
se tejen de plumas,
        y de andrajos;
se moldean de oro,
        y de barro;
se labran de jade,
        y de pómez.
Envejecer, atar la cosecha
de los años, contarlos—
es un arte—
        sea ya arte bueno o malo.
Sólo el pasar de los años,
tomar el rojo, el amarillo,
el negro, el blanco
no asegura que pintemos bien las cosas,
no nos hace de jade el corazón
no lo endiosa—
Para llegar al centro de piedra verde
depende sólo de que tan bien
aprendimos a amar,
lo capaces que fuimos en decirlo.

3 TOLTECUEUETIA: THE ART OF AGING

It is said that aging is an art—
the moments that give form to the years
        are composed, woven,
        molded, carved
They are composed of flower & song,
        & of thorn & weeping;
they are woven of plumes,
        & of rags;
they are molded of gold,
        & of clay;
they are carved of jade,
        & of pumice.
Aging, tying the harvest
of the years, counting them—
is an art—
        be it good art or bad.
The passing of the years alone,
taking the red, the yellow,
the black, the white
does not insure that we paint things well,
does not make the heart of jade
does not make it god—
To reach the center of green stone
depends only on how well
we learned to love,
how capable we were in telling it.

Sólo así se forma un rostro, un corazón,
se obra como tolteca,
sólo así se hace buen arte
del envejecer.

Only thus does one form a face, a heart,
create like a Toltec,
only thus is good art made
        of aging.

4 QUILTICOYOTL ALZA FLOR Y CANTO

El décimo día del décimo mes
de la décima década del milenio
atando un haz de años
tres banderas quince puntos,
el viejo coyote aun meneando
su aun verde rabo,
inseguro de su maestría
de la tinta negra, la tinta roja,
si dueño de un rostro
        (de múltiples máscaras)
de un corazón
        (labrado de jade imperfecto),
alza flor y canto
para dar gracias al Sol y a la Tierra
padre, madre, los dioses, las diosas
por el don de la vida
        y su máximo adorno—
                el amor, la amistad.

4 QUILTICOYOTL RAISES FLOWER & SONG

On the tenth day of the tenth month
of the tenth decade of the millennium,
tying a sheaf of years
three flags fifteen dots,
the old coyote,
still wriggling
his still green tail,
unsure of his mastery
of the black ink, the red ink,
if master of a face
        (of many masks)
of a heart
        (carved of flawed jade),
raises flower & song
to thank the Sun & the Earth
father, mother, gods, goddesses
for the gift of life
        & its greatest adornment—
            love, friendship.

5 NAUI PANTLI: CUATRO BANDERAS

Se alzan, se despliegan, se plantan
cuatro banderas: la roja,
la amarilla, la negra, la blanca.
Marcan los rumbos,
        indican los años.
               Bajo ellas
flores se pizcan para hacer el canto,
plumas se cogen para adornar el camino,
oro se mina para formarse el rostro,
jade se busca para labrarse el corazón.
        Bajo ellas
lo más digno de celebrarse
es lo capaz que uno ha sido
        en amar.

5 NAUI PANTLI: FOUR FLAGS

Raised, unfurled, placed,
four flags: the red,
the yellow, the black, the white.
They mark the directions,
       indicate the years.
              Under them
flowers are picked to make song,
feathers gathered to adorn the way,
gold mined to form the face,
jade sought to carve the heart.
       Under them
most worthy to celebrate
is how able one has been
       to love.

6 TLAZOCAMATI: FUEGO DE AMAR

Traer las cuatro banderas
(la roja, la amarilla, la negra, la blanca)
y las cinco cuentas (de piedra verde, de oro,
de pedernal, de obsidiana, de barro)
a esta altura no es fácil.
Se marchitan la flores, se desgarran las plumas,
se gasta el oro, se astilla la piedra verde.
Se ponen las banderas
al este, al sur, al oeste, al norte;
en el centro se arreglan las cinco cuentas.
Se celebra la ceremonia,
se hace la penitencia,
se abre, se valora el corazón.
Se alza la flor y el canto,
se dan gracias a la vida.
La Tierra escucha.

6 TLAZOCAMATI: FIRE OF LOVING

To bring the four flags
(the red, the yellow, the black, the white)
& the five beads (of green stone, of gold,
of quartz, of obsidian, of clay)
to this height is not easy.
The flowers wilt, the feathers are tattered,
the gold is worn, the green stone chipped.
The flags are placed
to the east, the south, the west, the north;
in the center are arranged the five beads.
The ceremony is celebrated,
penance is made,
the heart is opened, appraised.
Flower & song are raised,
thanks is given to life.
The Earth listens.

MAXIPAQUI: BENDICIÓN

Que el sagrado maíz
te alumbre
       como oro
           el día
y que de copas de jade,
de piedra verde
brindes a la vida
y se te llene de flores
      y plumas
         el corazón

MAXIPAQUI: BLESSING

May the sacred corn
light
    like gold
          your day
& from cups of jade,
of green stone
may you toast life
& flowers
     & feathers
         fill your heart.

DESCENSO A MICTLAN
(viaje chamánico al inframundo)

Cruza el campo amarillo de cempoales.
Baja al reino de las sombras—es amplio, es estrecho.
Llegamos a la boca de la caverna de cavernas,
reino de Mictlantecuhtli, Mictlancihuatl,
Señor, Señora Muerte—
es amplio, es estrecho;
pasa, entra a la sala de flores amarillas,
        el cempoalxochitl, la flor perfecta,
        flor de muertos.

Pisamos, caminamos
     caminamos en lo sagrado
      cada paso es sagrado.
Pisamos en los rastros de nuestros antepasados
pisamos en las huellas de los ancianos,
      nuestras abuelas, nuestros abuelos,
      los ancianos:
           la gente del tambor
           la gente de la canoa
           la gente de las pirámides
           la gente de la lanza
           la gente de la lanzadera y del telar
           la gente del hoz y el arado
           nuestros ancianos, todos los clanes.

Nos enseñaron a ver;
nos enseñaron a no ver;
de ellos hemos aprendido a ver
aprendido a no ver.
Nos enseñaron a soñar;
nos enseñaron a temer;
mucho que aprender; mucho que desaprender.
Caminamos en sus huellas, caminamos en lo sagrado.

Caminamos, pisamos las huellas de nuestros ancestros,
nuestra parentela
el jaguar
el bisonte
el coyote
el oso
el salmón, la serpiente, el águila, el halcón,
lobo, mono, tortuga, rana, murciélago, tecolote,
pulpo, cangrejo, almeja, ostión.
Más y más allá caminamos:
la araña, la mariposa, la mosca, el ácaro, el coral,
amiba, paramecia, germen, virus—todos los clanes.
Nos enseñaron a ver, a vivir en el presente
a oler, a probar
a escuchar, a vivir en el presente.
Pisamos en sus huellas,
caminamos en lo sagrado—
toda nuestra parentela, todos los clanes.

Caminamos, pisamos las huellas de los ancestros,
nuestra parentela
    el helecho, la secuoya
    el pino, el roble
    el cactus, el mezquite
    la violeta, la rosa
    el higo, la parra, el trigo
    el maíz, el cardo, la hierba
    el hongo, el musgo, el liquen, el alga,
    el moho—todos los clanes.
Nos enseñaron a palpar,
a gozar plenamente en el ahora
        a encontrar el contento en el aquí.
Pisamos en sus huellas,
    caminamos en lo sagrado
        toda nuestra parentela, todos los clanes.

Caminamos, pisamos
        en las huellas de los ancestros, nuestra parentela:
            el granito, la arenisca
            el jaspe, la serpentina
            la turquesa, el pedernal
            el ópalo, el cuarzo
            el ágata, el jade
            el oro, el hierro, la plata
            el plomo, el cobre, el estaño,
peñasco, guija, arena, polvo—todos los clanes.
Nos enseñaron silencio, quietud;
    nos enseñaron a quedarnos, a estar.

Pisamos en sus huellas,
    caminamos en lo sagrado—
        toda nuestra parentela, todos los clanes.

    Es oscuro; es claro—
he aquí las raíces del Árbol de la Vida,
    el árbol de Tamoanchan.
Mira: riqueza, tesoro, nuestra herencia
Mira: teocuitlatl, oro, mierda de los dioses;
    chalchihuitl, jade, la piedra verde;
    quetzalli, plumas, las cosas preciosas;
    xochitl, flores, las raíces de las flores.
Regalos y cargas,
    lo útil, lo estorboso
        la medicina oscura, el veneno brillante.
Pizca y escoge: hay alegrías empoderantes.
        congojas inútiles hay;
necesidades verdaderas—claras y lindas como el agua
deseos verdaderos—rojos y jubilosos como el vino;
    necesidades falsas y fatales como arsénico
    deseos falsos y mortales como cuchillos;
espadas con joyas,
    arados sucios y desafilados por las rocas,
    polvos deslumbrantes, hierbas ricas en visiones.
Escoge y separa—no es mucho lo que puedas llevar.

Los ancestros, nuestra parentela aconsejan; escucha:

Mucho nos han dejado nuestras madres, nuestros padres
    nuestras abuelas, nuestros abuelos
    nuestros ancestros.

he aquí dones para nuestra bendición
he aquí deudas para nuestra maldición.

Interroga a los ancianos—son sabios, son necios:
Señores míos, Señoras mías—
¿Qué verdades dicen sus flores, sus cantos?
¿Son verdaderamente bellas, ricas sus plumas?
¿No es el oro sólo excremento de los dioses?
Sus jades, ¿son los más finos, los más verdes?
Su legado, ¿es tinta negra, tinta roja?

Nos ofrecen dones, nos dan enseñanzas:
    preciosas, sin valor
    sanadoras, peligrosas—

Separa, escoge—escoge lo precioso, lo sano
              deja lo sin valor, lo dañoso
hay mucho que aprender, mucho que desaprender.
Escoge—cada cual ofrece dones,
los ancestros, nuestra parentela: humana,
    animal, vegetal, mineral—
son nosotros mismos, nuestra parentela.
Escoge y separa, separa y escoge—
    estos dones son de la Tierra
    estos dones la celebran y la nutren
    estos dones la blasfemen y la destruyen.
        Estos dones son de la Tierra.
Separa y escoge, escoge y separa.
Los ancianos son sabios, los ancianos son necios;
    riquezas recogieron, basura acumularon.
Acepta sólo lo preciso:

lo que te haga amplio el corazón
        lo que te ilumine el rostro.
Escoge y elige—
        calla—
en silencio separa y escoge, separa y escoge.

Calla—
        mira atentamente—¿hemos escogido bien?
el camino de regreso es duro, lleno de temor
        y mucho nos han dejado los ancestros.
¿Cuáles de sus dones son dignos de compartir?
        Piénsalo bien—
                el oro y la espada con joyas
no valen más que el arado desafilado por el trabajo.
Considera, comprueba tu decisión—

                                calla—

Nos esperan tareas en la Tierra para nuestro sanar,
        el sanar de ella—
                difíciles, grandes.
        Escoge bien para la jornada, para la labor.
Calla—
        recuerda:
la alegría es la raíz de nuestro poder,
las raíces que nos nutren vienen del corazón,
la ciencia más sabia perturba menos—

        calla—calla—calla

Bien, escogemos lo que escogemos;
Recuerda: de estos dones hacemos los nuestros;
      añadimos al montón;
      no cargues a los niños.
No cargues tanto
que no podamos cogernos de la mano.

      Recuerda: el tesoro más precioso
        es el que tomamos para el regalar.
Escogemos lo que escogemos—
      prepara—toma tu bulto,
las semillas de nuestro ser—es liviano, es pesado;
preciosos son los huesos de los ancestros;
dejarlos enterrados no los hacen menos preciosos;
son de la Tierra, Madre Tierra, Pachamama,
      Tonantzin: la Tierra los necesita.
      ehecatl, aire
      tletl, fuego
      atl, agua
      tlalli, tierra.

Prepárate a dejar el almacén, el tesoro;
camina alrededor de la caverna un vez más
como voltea el reloj:
      del este, rojo y dorado con sabiduría
      al sur amarillo y verde con amor
      al oeste negro y azul con fuerza
      al norte blanco con sanar.
Estás ya en el umbral—
      es amplio, es estrecho
      es oscuro, es claro

es empinado, es plano.
No mires hacia atrás;
deja Mictlan, reino de la muerte;
deja la caverna de los ancianos,
la cueva de nuestro tesoro;
comienza el camino de regreso.
Lo que se trae del reino de los muertos,
de entre los huesos de los ancestros,
es nuestro regalo a la vida.
Ruega a los dioses que hayas escogido bien.

Vuelve, vuelve.

Es tu compromiso
el sanarte a sí mismo y a la Tierra.
¿Qué harás?
¿Cómo honrarás a los ancestros?
¿Qué les dirás a los niños?
¿Qué harás por la justicia y la paz?

Vuelve, vuelve.

Vete—
lleva la bendición de la vida.

Vete—
forma un rostro, un corazón
in ixtli, in yollotl

Vete—
que los dioses te tengan.

Hagas lo que hagas, bendice a la vida.

Ve y pasa la bendición de la vida;

Vete, ha acabado; vete, el viaje a acabado—

Ve y empieza un día nuevo.

Regresa a tu mundo.

DESCENT TO MICTLAN
(shamanic journey to the underworld)

Cross the yellow fields of marigolds.
Descend to the realm of shadows - it is wide, it is narrow.
We come to the mouth of the cavern of caverns,
realm of Mictlantecuhtli, Mictlancihuatl,
Our Lord, Our Lady of Death—
It is wide, it is narrow;
enter this chamber of yellow blooms,
        the marigold, the perfect flower,
           flower of the Dead.

We step, we walk
    we walk the sacred
        every step is sacred.
We walk in the tracks of our ancestors'
we step in the tracks of the old ones,
    our grandmothers, our grandfathers,
    the ancients:
        the people of the drum
        the people of the canoe
        the people of the pyramids
        the people of the spear
        the people of the shuttle and loom
        the people of the sickle and plow
        our ancient ones, all of the clans.

They taught us to see;
they taught us not to see;
      from them we learned to see
                 we learned not to see.
They taught us to dream;
     they taught us to fear;
        much to learn, much to unlearn.
We step in their tracks, we step on the sacred.

We walk, we step in the tracks of our ancestors,
    our relations
       the jaguar
       the buffalo
       the coyote
       the bear
       the salmon, the serpent, the eagle, the hawk
       wolf, monkey, turtle, frog, bat, owl
       octopus, crab, oyster, clam.
Further, further we walk:
the spider, the moth, the fly, the coral, the mite,
amoeba, paramecium, germ, virus - all of the clans.
They taught us to see, to live in the now
    to touch, to smell, to taste
    to hear, to see.
We step in their tracks,
    we walk on the sacred -
       all our relations, all of the clans.

We walk, we step in the tracks of our ancestors,
our relations
        the fern, the redwood,
        the pine, the oak,
        the cactus, the mesquite,
        the violet, the rose,
        the fig, the grape-vine, the wheat,
        the corn, the thistle, the grass,
        the mushroom, the moss, the lichen, the algae,
        the mold—all of the clans.
They taught us to touch,
    to fully delight in the now
                    to find contentment on the here.
We step in their tracks,
            we walk on the sacred -
                    all our relations, all of the clans.

We walk, we step
in the tracks of our ancestors, our relations:
        the granite, the sandstone
        the jasper, the serpentine
        the turquoise, the flint
        the opal, the quartz
        the agate, the jade
        the gold, the iron, the silver
        the lead, the copper, the tin,
boulder, pebble, sand, dust—all of the clans.
They taught us silence, quiet;
        they taught us to stay, to be.

We step in their track,
    we walk on the sacred—
        all our relations, all of the clans.

    it is dark; it is light—
here the roots of the Tree of Life,
    the tree of Tamoanchan.
Look: wealth, treasure, our inheritance
Look: teocuitlatl, oro, gold, shit of the gods;
    chalchihuitl, jade, the green stone
    quetzalli, feathers, the precious things;
    xochitl, flowers, the roots of flowers.
Gifts and burdens,
    the useful, the hindering

    the dark medicine, the glittering poison.
Pick and choose: empowering joys there are
    useless sorrows there are;
needs true—clear and lovely as water
desires true—ruddy and joyous as wine;
    needs false and deadly as arsenic
    desires false and deadly as knives;
jeweled swords,
    plows muddied and dulled by stones,
    dazzling powders, herbs rich in visions.
Choose and sort—it is not much you can carry.

Our ancestors, our relations make council; listen:

Much have our mothers, our fathers left us
        our grandmothers, our grandfathers
        our ancestors.
                gifts are there for our blessing
                debts are there for our curse.

Question the ancients—they are wise, they are fools:
My Lords, my Ladies,
What truths do your flowers, your songs tell?
Are your feathers truly lovely, truly rich?
Is not gold only the excrement of the gods?
Your jades, are they the finest, the most green?
Your legacy, is it black ink, red ink?

They offer gifts, they give teachings:
        precious, worthless
        healing, dangerous—

Sort, choose—choose the precious, the whole;
                discard the worthless, the harmful
there is much to learn, much to unlearn.
Choose—each offers gifts,
the ancestors, our relations: human,
        animal, plant, mineral—
                they are us, our relations.
Choose and sort, sort and choose—
        these gifts are of the Earth
        these gifts celebrate and nurture her
        these gifts blaspheme and destroy her.
                These gifts are of the Earth.
Sort and choose, choose and sort.

The ancients are wise, the ancients are fools;
    riches they gathered, garbage they hoarded.
Accept only the necessary:
    what will widen your heart
        what will enlighten your face.
Pick and choose—
    shush—
in silence sort and choose, sort and choose.

Shush—
    Look carefully—have we chosen well?
the way back is hard, full of dread
    and much have our ancestors left us.
What of their gifts is worth the sharing?
        Consider well—
           the gold and the jeweled sword
are not worth more than the work-dulled plow.
Consider, test your choice—

                      shush—

Tasks await us on the Earth for our healing,
    her healing—
        difficult, great.
        Choose well for the journey, for the work.
Shush—
        remember:
joy is the root of our power,
the roots that feed us come from the heart
the science most wise disturbs least—

    shush—shush—shush

So, we choose what we choose;
Remember: from these gifts we make our own;
      we add to the pile;
            do not burden the children.
Do not carry so much
we cannot hold each other's hands.

      Remember: the most precious treasure
           is that which we take for the giving.
We choose what we choose—
      make ready—take up your bundle,
the seeds of our making—it is light, it is heavy;
precious are the bones of our ancestors;
leaving them buried makes them no less precious;
they are of the Earth, Madre Tierra, Pachamama,
      Tonantzin; the Earth needs them.
        ehecatl, air
        tletl, fire
        atl, water
        tlalli, earth.

Make ready to leave the store house, the treasure;
walk round the cavern once more
as the clock turns:
      from the East red and gold with knowledge
      to the South yellow and green with love
      to the West black and blue with strength
      to the North white with healing.
You are now at the threshold—
      it is wide, it is narrow
      it is dark, it is light
      it is steep, it is plane.

Do not look back;
leave Mictlan, realm of the dead;
    leave the cave of the ancients,
        the cave of our treasure;
    begin the way back.
What is brought back from the land of the dead,
    from among the bones of the ancestors,
        is our gift to life.
Pray the gods you choose well.

Return, return.

It is your commitment,
        the healing of yourself and the Earth.
What will you do?
        How will you honor the ancestors?
            What will you say to the children?
        What will you do for justice and peace?

Return, return.

Go—
take the blessing of life.

        Go—
                form a face, form a heart
                    in ixtli, in yollotl

Go—
may the gods keep you.

Whatever you do, bless life, bless life.

Go and pass on the blessing of life.

Go, it is finished; go, the journey is finished—

Go and begin a new day.

     Return to your world.

FLOWER OF GREEN STONE:

Metaphor of Nahua Poetry of Pre-Hispanic Mexico

According to Fray Diego Durán, referring to the Nahuas in the 16th century shortly after the defeat of Tenochtitlan, "All the poems of these [peoples] are composed of such obscure metaphors there are scarcely those who understand them unless they have very deliberately studied and analyzed them in order to understand their sense. I have set myself to deliberately listen with great attention to what they sing, and to the words and terms of the metaphors and they seemed to me nonsense, yet afterwards, speaking about them and discussing them, I have found them to be most admirable utterances."[1] And this judgment has changed very little in the years that separate Fray Diego and the contemporary student of the poetry of pre-Hispanic Mexico.

What confused the astute priest and scholar was not the language, which he had completely mastered but the metaphors of which the poetry was composed. Understanding is often very difficult as meaning forms slowly in the entrails of a culture, and mind and heart must leap over obstacles of ethnocentrism often insurmountable.

The language of the Nahuas is itself metaphorical, that is to say, based in symbol or at least description such that even if one knows the equivalent in Spanish or in English of a Nahuatl word so much is

---

1. Fray Diego Durán, *Historia de los indios de Nueva España e islas de Tierra Firme. México, 1867-80. José F. Ramírez, Vol. II, p. 233*

lost in the translation that everything save the most basic significant sense is lost. One such word is *centzontli*, which means the mocking bird. *Centzontli* literally means "bird of four-hundred voices," or bird of a thousand voices as the Nahuas used "four-hundred" as the Greeks used myriad to express any extraordinary number. Another is the verb *ixtlamachiliztli*, "to teach" which literally means "to give wisdom to the faces of others," something more specific and at the same time more complex than what the verb to teach means to us.

But it is not our interest here to get into the linguistic difficulties of the tongue of the Aztecs but to treat solely the proper metaphor, the metaphor used primarily for poetic expression in works of art.

At first sight, this would not appear so difficult but we must realize that the Nahua metaphor comes from a mythic-religious tradition vast and complex, a tradition so profound that until relatively recently have we begun to understand it and the influence it has had in the Mexican character. To attempt to explain or even suggest the meaning of all metaphor in Nahua poetry would require a study of this mythology and the philosophy and mysticism it contains, a task impossible to accomplish within the limits of many volumes. For which reason we will limit ourselves to the discussion of only four of the most used Nahua metaphors: flowers, plumes, jade (green stone), and the heart.

Even this study limited to only four metaphors takes us into the Aztec religion. Let us begin with an analysis of Xochipilli, Prince of Flowers, the Nahua god of Spring who is also the god of poetry and song. In the *Códice matritense del Real Palacio* in Madrid, the appearance of the god is described thus:

He is stained light red,
his facial make-up simulates weeping,
his hat with crest of red bird plumes.
He has his lip-plug of precious stones,
his collar of jade.
His strips of paper over the breast,
his loin cloth with red border.
His bells, his sandals with flowers,
His shield with solar design in turquoise mosaic at one side,
A staff with heart tip crested with quetzal.[2]

The Nahua peoples formed their cult principally around Ometeotl, the Dual God/Goddess, Creator of Life. Thus it was the most natural thing for them to adopt the Sun, origin of light and of life, as the visible symbol of life. (The Aztecs called themselves "The People of the Sun" to mean that they were the chosen.)

As Professor Miguel León Portilla says, Xochipilli represents the new sun, that is to say, Spring and the rebirth of the earth after winter.[3] The weeping of the god in this instance does not denote sorrow but the rebirthing rains of the season at the same time that the solar symbol of turquoise mosaic on his shield identifies him as a solar deity.

The name Xochipilli means "Prince of Flowers" and the flower is found in the decoration of his sandals. Flowers were sacred to the Nahuas as the manifestation of the rebirth of life and the first stage in the development of fruit, the sustenance of life. As we present symbolic keys to distinguished visitors to our cities, the Nahuas presented them cones and wreaths of flowers. The phrase "flowery War" designated the ritual wars in search of victims for the sacrifice that the Aztecs waged

---

2. Miguel León-Portilla, *Ritos, sacerdotes y atavíos de los dioses,* Universidad Nacional Autónoma de México, 1958. p. 149
3. *Ibid. (note 47)*

against neighboring kingdoms. "Flowery" applied to war came from the belief that warriors acquired honor in these battles and if they died would be reborn as birds and butterflies in the paradise of the Sun as would the victims of sacrifice and women dying in child-birth (others went to lesser worlds.)

Apart from these connotations of worth that the flower had for the Nahuas, flowers came to be the specific metaphor for poetry. Ángel María Garibay K. the foremost authority on Nahuatl poetics, says that the phrase "flower and song" that so often appears in pre-Hispanic literature means poetry.[4] The custom of the Nahuas of coupling two images to express a concept that would stir "in the human mind a vision—not abstract and cold as in the Aristotelian idea—but rich in content, alive, dynamic, and at the same time possessing a universal worth"[5] came from a fecund imagination and an intuition for symbols of ingenious appropriateness and richness. The riotous burst of flowers and volley of song from the mating birds at spring must have seemed to these ancient people most similar to poetic inspiration both for sweetness and spontaneity, for even as the seemingly sudden explosion of color in the blooms of spring was secretly developed in the dark womb of winter, so was the smooth flow of poetry first formed in the obscure precincts of the poet's heart.

In the many codices (the painted books of the early Mexicans) we may see the meaning that the flower had for them. In their system of pictographs or glyphs, to write that a man spoke, they painted the picture of the man, a bit of vapor issuing from his lips. To denote that what he said was particularly beautiful or truthful, they painted the speech-scroll with blossoms.

The poem "Beginning of Song" is easily understood in this light.

---

4. Ángel María Garibay K., *Llave del Náhuatl*, Otumba, México 1940, p. 112
5. Miguel León Portilla, *La filosofía Náhuatl estudiada en sus fuentes*, Instituto Indigenista Interamericano, México 1956, p. 176

What may have at one time been taken by the Spaniards as a flow-er-picking song is in fact a poem about poetry.[6]

> I ask my heart:
> "Where shall I pick the beautiful and fragrant blooms?
> Whom shall I ask?
> Shall I perhaps ask the brilliant green sucker of roses,
> The emerald fly-bird? Shall I perhaps ask the golden butterfly?
> Yes, they will know: they know where
> the beautiful and fragrant flowers open their crowns.

Among the so-called "secular" poems of the Mexicans those of friend-ship, war, *ubi sunt, carpe diem*, and *ars poetica* abound. Of these, it seems, the poem about poetry predominates, perhaps because it so often contains in itself themes of the others. At any rate, we can be very sure that the Nahuas were obsessed by the magic of words, the sacredness of speech (it was a custom that before speaking or singing in public, the nobles and priests burned copal, incense, in preparation for that sacred act) and explored the intricacies of language in their poetry, limited though it may have been by a highly formulaic tradition and structured system of myth.

One such poem is the "Song of Cuacuauhutzin," by one of the poet-kings of ancient Mexico, In this particular work, as in quite a few others, it is evident that the Nahuas recognized the part pain often plays in the creation of poetry:[7]

> Deeply yearn for flowers, my heart!
> Songs pain me. I only rehearse them on this earth:

---

6. Ángel María Garibay K., *Poesía indígena,* Universidad Nacional Autónoma de México 1952, p. 67

7. Ángel María Garibay K., *Poesía Náhuatl,* Universidad Nacional Autónoma de México, 1964, Vol. I, p. 69

128

I, Cuacuahutzin.
I would that flowers lasted in my hand!
Where shall I gather the beautiful flowers and songs?

Here the spring never bears them forth.
I only torment myself, I, Cuacuahutzin.
Can we rejoice, I wonder? Can my friends find joy?
Where shall I gather the beautiful flowers and songs?

Another symbol favorite of the Nahuas was the quetzal plume. In Nahuatl, the word quetzal also means "precious" so that such images as "quetzalxóchitl" can be interpreted both as "precious flower" or "flower of plumes." Monsignor Garibay defines the term "jade and fine feathers" as meaning riches.[8] These feathers were one of the most highly prized materials of the Aztecs; the crowns, scepters, and capes of their emperors were fashioned of them and they formed part of the attire of their gods.

The Spaniards with their taste for gold appear absurd even to the westerner when viewed through the eyes of the Mexicans:

> They picked up the gold and fingered it like monkeys; they seemed to be transported by joy, as if their hearts were illumined and made new.
> The truth is that they longed and lusted for gold. They snatched at the golden ensigns, waved them from side to side and examined every inch of them. They were like one who speaks a barbarous tongue: everything they said was in a barbarous tongue.

---

8. Ángel María Garibay K., op cit. *Llave del Náhuatl*

* * *

The Spaniards immediately stripped the feathers from the gold shields and ensigns. They gathered all the gold into a great mound and set fire to everything else, regardless of its value. Then they melted down the god into ingots. As for the precious jades, they took only the best of them; the rest were snatched by the Tlaxcaltecas. [9]

This is the picture we get through the incredulous eyes of a people who valued the quetzal and jade as much if not more than the yellow metal. The conquistadores' barbarous disregard for the beauty of the Aztecs' works of art appalled the Mexicans, who, helpless, saw their precious feather crowns and banners destroyed. But though our museums are destitute of these marvelous creations, the tradition of their worth and beauty comes down to us through the poetry of the Nahuas where feathers always denote something of great beauty and price. [10]

Where do you walk, oh poet?
Let the flowered tambourine be prepared,
ringed with quetzal plumes, adorned with flowers of gold
to delight the nobles, the princes,
the Eagle and Ocelot knights.

An even more prized possession of the Mexicans was the green stone or jade, the sacred gem of Tlaloc, so holy and potent that a bead of it conceived Quetzalcoatl in the womb of his mother who had swallowed it. This jewel was the token of all that was sacred, noble, linked

9. Miguel León Portilla, *Visión de los vencidos: Relaciones indígenas de la conquista*, UNAM México 1969; p. 53 y 71
10. Ángel María Garibay K., *op cit. Poesía indígena*, p. 83

with life. In the sacred city of Teotihuacan, in Tetitla, a mural in the entrance porch to the patio depicts the rain god Tlaloc dropping gifts in the form of precious jade objects—these gifts are those of life itself, for the Nahuas saw in the muted greens of jade the light of life intuited in the quickening sap at the crack of spring. From urns of jade Tlaloc sent his life-engendering rains. When someone died, a piece of jade was placed in his or her mouth to take the place of the heart which had lost its beat. "The gold crown and jade earrings of his exalted office" were the only accoutrements that identified Motecuhzoma in the austerity of his council chamber.[11]

It is little wonder that the Aztecs thought the Spaniards barbarians to despise their sacred chalchíhuitl which Brinton defines as "the famous 'green-stone' or jade so highly prized by the Mexicans; often used figuratively for anything noble, beautiful and esteemed."[12] For the Aztecs, gold was valued only as a setting and enhancement for the sacred substance as an Otomí song demonstrates:

> My song is polished jade
> and molded gold;
> I make a setting for jade;
> the setting is my song.

This short verse is more subtle than first appears. To begin with, the Nahuatl metaphors or symbols fell into a hierarchy, as for example, flowers, feathers, gold, and jade. Each was precious and a symbol of preciousness, but each was limited by its nature; feathers outlast flowers, gold outlasts feathers, and jade outlasts gold. Irene Nicholson astutely noted this in her book, *Firefly in the Night*:

---

11. G. C. Vaillant, *The Aztecs of Mexico*, Penguin Books, 1960, p. 222
12. D. G. Brinton, *Ancient Náhuatl Poetry*, Philadelphia, 1887, p. 130

> Jewels, as well as flowers, were a favorite symbol of
> the Nahuas, and it looks very much as if jewels and flowers
> were both used to represent the heart-made-god, but at
> different stages of the process. Flowers fade and die, they
> are not permanent; but jewels have a longer life than many
> generations of men. It is probable, therefore, that whenever
> we find a jewel mentioned in the poetry it signifies a more
> permanent achievement of the human being.[13]

Now the apparently simple verse begins to take on more subtle shadings. The song, the poetic expression of the Otomí or noble is likened to a jewel of jade meaningful with the very essence of life and eternal, but the poet realizes that the song itself is not what is eternal, but the thing it expresses, the fecundity of the singer's heart so that the song, beautiful as it may be, is only a setting for the more precious jade of the poet's consciousness of life.

This brings us to the fourth symbol, the heart, possibly the most telling symbol comprising the dress of Xochipilli. The young god carries on his person the flower, the quetzal plume and the jade collar, but perhaps the heart on his baton is what gives him his stature, for in the Nahua pantheon as compiled by León-Portilla, Xochipilli and Macuilxochitl (who is considered the same god as Xochipilli by another name) are the only two gods who have the heart as part of their person. To realize how important this is we must recall that the highest tribute the Aztecs could make their gods was the human heart, the center of feeling and courage and knowledge. We must not allow custom nor our personal repugnance for blood-shed (I say personal, for our history of

---

13. Irene Nicholson, *Firefly in the Night*, London, 1959, p. 159

continual wars including our present ones prevents us from calling it natural or cultural) keep us from understanding that this ancient culture recognized the human consciousness and being as the most precious of things, the most worthy immolation for their gods.

The Aztecs had two types of colleges or schools, the Telpochcalli for the common people and the Calmecac for the princes and the gifted, noble or not. Two languages were taught, one for the common people at the Telpochcalli and one (called tecpilatilli, that is, "noble and cultivated tongue") for the nobles at the Calmecac. This "noble tongue" was a refined Nahuatl abounding in formulas of courtesy and protocol that were employed not only for grace and beauty of manner but for more telling speech and communication on more delicate and subtle levels. One of the formulas frequently found in this refined speech is the term in ixli in yollotl ("your face, your heart") and is used always as a metaphor for what we may now call "the integral character of a human being," that is, the harmony between the external act of a person and the intimate psychological motivation within him or her which constitutes his or her personality. In addressing another person with this formula, one was formally recognizing in him or her the most important attribute of a mature person (omacic oquichtli), that he or she is "master of a face and a heart," that he or she has integrity.

This is the key to an understanding of the Nahua concept of the human. One of the words for teacher, *teixcuitiani*, means "one-who-makes-others-take-on-a face," that is, makes them define their characters, or if you will, discover themselves. But this is only part of the teacher's duty to "humanize people," for the Nahuas said that "thanks to him, the love of the people is humanized" (*itech netlacaneco*) because he "makes the hearts strong" (*tlayolpachivitia.*) León-Portilla defines the word literally thus: Composed of tla- prefix of undefined character which connotes a relationship with "the most varied things or circumstances"; yol(otl: heart); pachivitia (to make strong). Putting together these diverse elements: tla-yol-pachivitia signifies "make hearts strong with relation to things."[14]

To "make hearts strong with relation to things" is easy enough to understand, not at all easy to define, and most difficult to achieve. What the Nahuas must have meant by this term can be found by piecing together the scattered mosaics of their thought as found in what remains of their literature. Another of the attributes of the mature person is that he or she has a "heart firm like stone." In our own culture we have the term "heart of stone" meaning an unfeeling, cruel character. But this is not at all what the Nahuas meant. The world yóllotl, heart, comes from ollin, movement. This movement is indicative of life. When "stone" (supreme stillness) is coupled with "heart" (source of movement), we get an image of dynamic stability, and when this stability is "strong with relation to things," we get something like the "unmoving mover" principle of Eastern mysticism—a consciousness existing in and with the varied forces of the human condition, yet master of itself.

This concept is made even more complex and subtle when we get the metaphor of the "jade heart, green stone" the stable heart whose stability issues from the very substance of which it is formed, life, the source of movement which must simultaneously be still and moving in perfection—a perfection not to be reached perhaps, but to be constantly sought.

This symbol of the jade heart, heart of green stone is probably related to the symbol of Quetzalcoatl, the Plumed Serpent. In the Plumed Serpent are brought together two diverse principles which we can call the male and the female—Yin-Yang. In Nahua mythology the serpent is always identified with the Mother Goddess (Coatlicue), the Earth, the female principle. The bird, on the other hand, is iden-

---

14. Miguel León-Portilla, *Siete ensayos sobre cultura Náhuatl*. Universidad Nacional Autónoma de México 1958, p. 69

tified with masculinity (Huitzilopochtli), the sky, the heroic. In the feathered snake the two principles are united: the serpent with the possibility of flight and the bird who must not lose contact with the Earth. Psychologically this is a perfect symbol. The intrusive tendency for abstraction, idealization, high-flown adventure we associate with the male is balanced by the inclusive tendency toward the personal, the concrete, the closeness to the hearth that we associate with the female. It was this ideal, personified, that became the patron god of culture, art, knowledge.

Language is a most intricate and dangerous tool. With it we must capture truth. Words are so many hands with which we must grasp the great butterfly. If we hold it too tightly, we mutilate it; if we hold it too lightly it escapes us. The Nahuas very wisely let it fly between their compound terms such as "flower and song," "jade and fine feathers," "face and heart," trusting that somewhere between the two words one could catch a glimpse of the truth, knowing that its movement and flight were as much a part of itself as the chemical composition of its wings.

Ours is a poverty-stricken age, as Thomas Wolfe would have it, "poverty-stricken in symbols." In our zeal for the total control of the Earth, we have become satisfied with the purely palpable and measurable part of existence and disregarded the rest. We delude ourselves that the lifeless tissue of the butterfly wing beneath our microscopes is the butterfly and our vision becomes ever more limited as humanity quests for reality in such narrow straits. Susanne Langer tells us in *Philosophy in a New Key*, "since he has learned to esteem signs above symbols, to suppress his emotional reactions in favor of practical ones and make use of nature instead of holding so much of it sacred, he has altered the face, if not the heart of reality." And Gerald Vann in *The Water and the Fire* observes that we

... live in a lopsidedly cerebral age: the vast triumphs of science have caused us to neglect and perhaps to deride the other avenues of knowledge; we make use of symbols of course, but for the most part they are strictly practical and utilitarian, like the road signs or the barber's pole; the rest is largely lost. There are poets still, but few are interested to read them; there are artists still, but few are concerned to understand them, there are wise men, but few have time to listen to them.[15]

Time was the preoccupation of the Nahuas. They had measured it with such perfection, not to hoard and save as in our age, but to gain wisdom from it. It has been found that the Nahua culture had the wheel and knew its use. But, in what may seem to us folly, they never adopted it technically to save time or labor. They used it ceremoniously in the rituals to their gods or for the toys of their children.

But it is not technology that the student of pre-Hispanic Mexico seeks to learn from Nahua poetics, but the secret of language, the truths (not facts) encased in its complex and faceted metaphors which have formed so much a part of the Mexican identity. In order to understand it we must become aware of our own limitations and blind spots.

In the present world we are about to lose it all. We use our science and technology to abuse one another and Mother Earth herself. We have a very petty sense of values, benighted, foolish, and are about to lose it all—the Mother Earth herself that gives us birth and sustains us. I do not say that poetry is our salvation, but through it we may begin to recognize the sacredness of life and the Earth. And most especially

15. Gerald Vann, *The Water and the Fire*, New York 1954, p. 16

the poetry of those indigenous cultures that we of the Western world in our blind arrogance have tried to completely destroy in the five-hundred-twenty-five some odd years of conquest and colonization of the Americas. Let us hope that it not be too late, and cultivating the heart of jade, make our hearts god and realize the sacredness of Life, of the Earth that birthed and sustains it.

READING GUIDE

Theme: *Every Language Is A World*

Every culture, every language is a world in itself, a way of looking at and creating reality. Chalchiuixochitl/Flor de Piedra Verde/Flower of Jade is an attempt to recreate the Nahua world, the Nahua people's way of looking at things.

Shortly after the fall of Tenochtitlan to the Spaniards in 1521, Fray Bernardino de Sahagún, a scholar from the University of Salamanca, sought to record the world of the Nahuas by interviewing the wise elders of the fallen empire. The record of his research, The Florentine Codex, encompasses many books. Book 11 consists of the definitions of "Earthly Things" by the elders. Most things have more than one aspect, some contradictory. The poem "Calli: casa, house," defines "house" as a Nahua person might have done.

Representative Poems

1. "Ayacachtli: Sonaja, Rattle,"
2. "Centli: maíz, Corn,"
3. "Papalotl: mariposa, Butterfly"

Prompt:

- Can you write a poetic definition of something seen through your own eyes?
- Can you write a poetic definition of something as it might be seen through the eyes of the Nahua people or of any other people not of the English tradition

Theme: Two Images to Represent A Single Thing

Many times, the Nahuas created terms of two words, *difrasismos*, that stood for a single thing such as "in xochitl in cuicatl," flower and song to mean "poem" or "poetry." Another is "in chalchihuitl in quetzalli," greenstone and fine feathers to mean something precious, valuable. "In ixtli in yollotl" face and heart means a whole person. And "in tlilli in tlapalli," red and black ink means writing. This occurs in all languages; in English "cap and grown" means academia and "bread and roses" means material and spiritual well-being.

Representative Poems

"In Xochitl in Cuicatl: Flor y Canto, Flower & Song,"
"Teixcuitiani: maestro, Teixcuitiani: Teacher,"
"Un sacerdote desterrado se dirige a Coatlicue, An Exiled Priest Addresses Coatlicue"

Prompt:

- Can you couple two words to stand for a single thing?

Theme: All Languages Use Metaphors

Poets (and everyone is a poet) of all cultures create metaphors, seeing something as alike and standing for something else. The Nahuas used flowers to stand for poetry, quetzal feathers to stand for riches. We often hear "money" referred to as "dough" or "bread." Those are metaphors. So is saying that the U.S.A. is a "melting pot" and saying that life is a "rollercoaster." A child poet said that the crescent moon is a yellow banana.

Representative Poems

> "Chalchiuhyollotl: Corazón de Piedra, Heart of Green Stone,"
> "Para el bautizo de un profeta/For the Baptism of a Prophet,"
> "Rezo a Tonantzin/Prayer to Tonantzin"

Prompt:

- Can you create a metaphor, name something that stands for something else?

Theme: *Metaphors Can Become Symbols*

Metaphors can often become symbols, evolve from comparing two different things to standing-in for something much more complex, multidimensional, meaning many things. The Nahuas use of "green-stone" to stand for life and for enlightenment is such an instance. The cross is a symbol for the Christian religion and for faith in all their complexity. The flag is a symbol for a whole nation and for patriotism in all their complication.

Representative Poems

"Yollotl: Corazón, Heart,"
"Ihiyotl: Aliento, Breath,"
"Nuestro movimiento, nuestra revolución;
Our Movement, Our Revolution"

Prompt:

- Can you create a symbol, think of a thing that can stand for something much bigger and complex?
- Can you write a poem using both metaphor and symbol?

ACKNOWLEDGMENTS

Were I to here acknowledge all who helped and inspired and had part in the creation of these poems, this book, the pages would exceed those of the book itself; tlazocamati, gracias, thank you from the heart.

That said, I would honor the memory of Leila Rae, my student, dear friend, publisher of Pandemonium Press, Berkeley, who insisted that I put my poems in the Nahua mode together and send them to Nomadic Press.

And I would be remiss not to mention J. K. Fowler, publisher of Nomadic Press and my editor Noelia Cerna with whom it was such a pleasure to work. tlazocamati, gracias, thank you.

Acknowledgements of published poems

Flower of Jade: Metaphor of Nahua Poetry of Pre-Hispanic Mexico; an earlier version was published in the *West Coast Review* vol. 4 no. 3, January 1970; author's copyrights.

Calli: Casa *El Hacedor de Juegos/The Maker of Games*; Casa Editorial; San Francisco 1977-78, first & second editions; author's copyrights.

Rafael Jesús González

Rafael Jesús González, Prof. Emeritus of literature and creative writing, was born and raised on the El Paso, Texas/Cd. Juárez, Chihuahua border. He taught at various universities before settling at Laney College, Oakland, California where he founded the Dept. of Mexican & Latin-American Studies 1969. He was Poet in Residence at Oakland Museum of California and Oakland Public Library 1996. Also a visual artist, his work has been exhibited at the Oakland Museum of California, and the Mexican Museum of San Francisco among others. Four times nominated for a Pushcart prize, he was honored for his writing by the National Council of Teachers of English 2003. He received a César Chávez Lifetime Achievement Award 2013 and one from the City of Berkeley in 2015. In 2017 he was named Berkeley's first Poet Laureate.

rjgonzalez.blogspot.com

COVER MISSIVE

On "Flower of green stone" glyph extrapolated from the image of Huehuecoyotl in the Codex Borbonicus
by Rafael Jesús González

Huehuecoyotl (Viejo Coyote), antiguo dios mexica de la poesía, música, danza, bordado y todas las artes. En el Códice Borbónico se representa bailando con una sonaja en la mano izquierda y en la mano derecha una flor la cual fue tomada y sobrepuesta en papel amate (papel en que los codices fueron pintados) para la cubierta del libro.

(El dibujo de Huehuecoyotl es por Rafael Jesús González)

Huehuecoyotl (Old Coyote), ancient Mexica god of poetry, music, dance, embroidery, and all the arts. In the Codex Borbonicus he is represented dancing with a rattle in his left hand and in his right hand a flower which was taken and superimposed on amate paper (paper on which the codices were painted) for the cover of the book.

(The drawing of Huehuecoyotl is by Rafael Jesús González)

Nomadic Press Emergency Fund

Nomadic Press Black Writers Fund

Right before Labor Day 2020 (and in response to the effects of COVID), Nomadic Press launched its Emergency Fund, a forever fund meant to support Nomadic Press-published writers who have no income, are unemployed, don't qualify for unemployment, have no healthcare, or are just generally in need of covering unexpected or impactful expenses.

Funds are first come, first serve, and are available as long as there is money in the account, and there is a dignity centered internal application that interested folks submit. Disbursements are made for any amount up to $300.

All donations made to this fund are kept in a separate account. The Nomadic Press Emergency Fund (NPEF) account and associated processes (like the application) are overseen by Nomadic Press authors and the group meets every month.

On Juneteenth (June 19) 2020, Nomadic Press launched the Nomadic Press Black Writers Fund (NPBWF), a forever fund that will be directly built into the fabric of our organization for as long as Nomadic Press exists and puts additional monies directly into the pockets of our Black writers at the end of each year.

Here is how it works:

$1 of each book sale goes into the fund.

At the end of each year, all Nomadic Press authors have the opportunity to voluntarily donate none, part, or all of their royalties to the fund.

Anyone from our larger communities can donate to the fund. This is where you come in!

At the end of the year, whatever monies are in the fund will be evenly distributed to all Black Nomadic Press authors that have been published by the date of disbursement (mid-to-late December).

The fund (and associated, separate bank account) has an oversight team comprised of four authors (Ayodele Nzinga, Daniel B. Summerhill, Dazié Grego-Sykes, and Odelia Younge) + Nomadic Press Executive Director J. K. Fowler.

Please consider supporting these funds. You can also more generally support Nomadic Press by donating to our general fund via nomadicpress.org/donate and by continuing to buy our books. As always, thank you for your support!

Scan the QR code for more information and/or to donate.

You can also donate at nomadicpress.org/store.